ZENITHITY AND THE RIDDLE OF DESTINY

Zenithity and the Riddle of Destiny
Jayce Dalton Free

Published by Dreams of Tigers
Atlanta, Georgia, USA

Additional copyright and background information can be found in the section after the index called:
"Copyright and Retitling Notes"

ISBN Paperback: 979-8-9992973-1-0
ISBN Ebook: 979-8-9992973-0-3

ZENITHITY AND THE RIDDLE OF DESTINY

JAYCE DALTON FREE

DREAMS
OF TIGERS

Contents

Copyright and Retitling Notes

Prior to its publication, this book was originally registered in the U.S. Copyright Office in 2023 as an unpublished work under the original draft title;

Ultramation and the Mechanysis of Perfunction: An Optimistic and Enduring Worldview

However, at the time of its initial publication in 2025, the title of the book was changed to:

Zenithity and the Riddle of Destiny: The Unfurling of the Conscious Future – A Metaphysical Journey

This is relevant because the primary philosophical concept described herein was originally called "Ultramation" when first drafted but is now called "Zenithity" throughout this book.

This book was extensively edited prior to publication in 2025, so it differs somewhat from the version that was originally sent to the U.S. Copyright Office prior to publication.

Other works previously published by Jayce Dalton Free, as well as numerous (often handwritten) draft essays dating back as early as 1979, still reference the originally coined word "Ultramation" as the name of the key theory or concept. Now the word "Ultramation" will instead be replaced by the word "Zenithity" in newly published books and other media.

For all intents and purposes, the two phrases are interchangeable, but the term Zenithity will be the preferred and more commonly used of these terms moving forward.

Introduction

At first, I was inclined to not do an introduction. I understand that most books do have one nowadays, and I have written several other books (mostly yet unpublished) – and each of them already has an introduction which has already been written. For *those* books I strongly consider the introduction to be an integral and indispensable part of the book itself.

But why should this book be required to have one, as it is a short book which is in essence itself but a summary, whose brief but abstract content defies further summarization? Better to dive right in fresh and start the journey with the narrative along the original path as was originally intended.

After all, did Voltaire or Dickens have to write an introduction? If we had to strike or burn every classic work for lack of an introduction (in their original editions), we might find ourselves sadly bereft of the very best of classical literature.

And no, I am not comparing myself to Voltaire, Dickens, or any of the great classic writers. I am simply trying to make a logical point, which is basically, "Why do we consider an introduction so darned important in the modern world?"

Anyway, my editor, in doing her due diligence (as she rightfully should), implored via a little note, which inquired, "Do you plan to do an introduction? An introduction can help you describe the book to your target audience."

"Target audience?" the marketing term stuck in my craw.

She knew I was having trouble defining a "target audience" for this book.

It was something we had discussed before, and a topic toward which I had acquired a bit of a mental block, or a revulsion perhaps, especially for a work of this nature.

Within the field of publishing, defining a target audience is basically the act of narrowing down a broad swath of people who 'should read' a particular book. For promotional purposes it helps to know which limited subset of people might want to read a given book.

"Target audience," I muttered aloud, half audible.

In my mind, anyone, or *everyone* could potentially read this book. There is no pre-defining set of characteristics that might predict who would or would not appreciate a book of this type – other than perhaps having a brain.

After ruminating on this idea for a few days, I grudgingly half-agreed to write an introduction. I must say that I "half-agreed" because I decided, in my contrarian fashion, to make an introduction that primarily describes not *who should read* the book, but more importantly, *who should not*.

So, here goes...

If you are a person who believes *only* in something that is derived from, or is supported by, some teaching that is rooted in an ancient "sacred" scripture of any type – *don't read this book.*

While this book may reference or parallel *some* teachings from *some* of these ancient teachings, it is neither the focus nor the intent of this book to subvert or redirect any line of thought, passion, or reason, simply because it does not proceed from, or align with, the teachings handed down by any ancient "gods".

So, if you are very content within your beliefs, and if your beliefs hinge ever so tightly upon the idea that they are correct because *you think* they were long ago handed down or somehow transcribed by an ancient god's ancient prophets – *then please do not read this book.* I do not wish to disrupt your faith and contentment in whichever beliefs you have chosen.

And if you are someone who strictly believes that there is *nothing* to this life but brick and stone, and all forms of dead matter without purpose, soul, or reasoning – then you might be offended by notions asserted herein. For example, the assertion that Life might represent something greater than an outgrowth from a piece of biodegradable matter – well, this might *offend* you. So, if any thought to the contrary upsets your sternly founded atheistic complacency – *then, please, don't read this book.* I really don't want to make you any more agitated than needs be.

And if you are someone who can't incorporate *anything* new; who upon hearing about any new thing can't possibly *consider* it (let alone begin to fathom incorporating it), then perhaps this book is not for you. If we can't, as people, engage in a conversation in which *either* side is ready or willing to at least entertain the mere possibility of changing, adapting, or enlarging their own static viewpoints, then what is the point of the conversation?

So if you are a person who has settled firmly within your own knowledge of all things, you have absolute contentment in your understanding of all things, and there is nothing new under the sun that can make you happier or more effective by one iota – *then, please, don't read this book.* For you, my friend, have already attained perfection, and I would urge you to write your own book which I would gladly read with an eager and open mind.

So, who's left?

And, so, we might toss our hands up to the sky at this point and ask, "Who's left?!"

If we have eliminated all people belonging strictly to any scriptural religion, and all persons who define themselves as hard core atheists, then basically who's left? Indeed, the "target audience" (did I mention this is a term I detest?) for this book is growing exceedingly slim.

But then I recalled, that in survey after survey, there is a huge section of people who self-identify, not as members of any specific religion, and not as atheistic or agnostic, but instead as belonging to a seemingly nebulous category defined as "spiritual but not religious." And when you look more closely, in countries or regions where a particular religion is not harshly forced upon people by society or strictly enforced by government authority, this category is as large if not larger than any of the sects or religions that were literally listed on the survey.

In fact, the "spiritual but not religious" segment of the population, in some countries (especially the more advanced countries), represents a *larger* segment of people than all religious and all non-religious people *combined*. On certain surveys, this alternative is not listed as one of the options, but whenever it *is* included (on surveys performed in advanced open societies), it is *always* one of the largest population segments.

On other surveys, it is a category with a different (but similar sounding) name or description, but when this option or a similar sounding option (like "spiritual but not affiliated") is omitted, there is a large surge in self-identification with a category that is simply called "other." Of course, don't we all have a pretty good idea, that when you list *all* the available religions, and then you list atheism and agnosticism, what exactly this "other" category entails? I think we all know that "other", in this context, is generally that same group of people who loosely identify as "spiritual but not religious", or "spiritual but not affiliated". Whatever that means, right?

What's going on here? Why are so many people having trouble identifying their beliefs (or identifying *with* their beliefs)?

Well, what's going on is that well-educated and thoughtful people worldwide are outgrowing the superstitious and often childlike narratives which dominate many of the outdated scriptures to which most "modern day" religions cling. Yet, those same people are not ready to ditch or boot the whole idea that there is something magnificent underlying and encompassing all of life, the universe, and everything. They still see that there is something beyond hard matter in this life and they recognize or even revere the elevated aspect of the human experience. There is a feeling or an awareness of something sublime even in the absence of the dictates of a scriptural or formal religion.

So, while this book was not originally written to "target" people in this large "middle ground" between the scriptural and the atheistic, it appears now (as I review the edited version) that it may, in fact, appeal most strongly to that ever so fuzzy "demographic." For while this book did not initially intend to "target" that group (or any specific group for that matter), it does *seem* to color-in some of the gray areas that were subtly or perhaps subconsciously lurking behind the logic and thinking of those within that vast group.

After reviewing everything through this lens, I realize this book might best appeal to those people who don't really fit the mold in many respects, and people who at best seem to fit the description of "other".

So, coming back around for another pass, and this time from the positive perspective;

If you are someone who is not *too easily* offended due to the rigidity of your own prior beliefs – you might actually enjoy this book.

If you are a human being who is interested in the great art of being human, you might find this book philosophically enticing and enriching.

And more specifically, if you find yourself interested in exploring the nature of consciousness, the future, and our ever-growing place in this phenomenological universe – then I would welcomingly say,

"This book's for you."

On the other hand, you might wish to pretend that this introduction never existed, as I had originally intended, and simply delve forward and forge, as always, ever ahead.

Either way, enjoy your journey!

All That Is and All That Will Be

Life and all the Universe had origins in an infinitely primal "moment." The word "moment" is used somewhat figuratively here, since there is no word to describe a *type* of moment that predates yet apparently emanates time itself. So, despite our latent incapacity to do so, we must conceive of something like a "meta-moment." This unique "instant" wherein time "began" perhaps consisted of yet another type of infinity within a mere blip of time apparent; instantaneous in one dimension, yet eternally long in our own.

But without some *form* of time already in existence, this supposed "initial" event seemingly cannot happen. Without time, there is nothing "before" and nothing can "begin". The idea of time "beginning" *implies* time already existing, or else "when" does it "start"?

It likewise feels inconceivable that time would have always existed, but this may be a *slightly* more comprehensible paradigm since if it "always" existed, it never needed to "begin" at some point in *time* (which by definition had not yet existed).

Regardless, this quandary is an enigma beyond the comprehension of those of us who are *bound within* the web of time's ceaseless flow. Since this is the only form of awareness I have ever known (that I can recall), we shall move forward from considering absolute antiquities.

Regardless of its origins, or the lack thereof into prior perpetuity, we could say that time has apparently flowed onward rather reliably ever since.

From then on, through and via the long and steady march of time, the conditions regarding the evolvement and refinement of Life have been arguably quite progressive. Life, along with the associated consciousness that we know, and all the higher variants of consciousness that are both known and unknown to us, have unfolded or will unfold, all in their due time. It is this great unfurling and refinement of the conscious element that is, in one sense, the "purpose" of time and the universe, for Life surpasses or transcends all of the dead matter throughout the cosmos.

For Life, and the Universe which bears it, are inextricably bound to, and tend toward, a *future* which embodies the Ultimate. An inevitable 'paradise,' if you will, an ultimate refinement of all things, awaits us as we progressively gravitate toward the inescapable yet paramount conclusion. For

Life, Consciousness, once born and since thriving, now exerts its growing influence upon the course of events. This is as willed by the net sum of Consciousness, embedded now partly within matter ("The-All"), which should (and does) assert its influence over matter, over time.

As such, "God" (in this context "pure Consciousness" or a more elemental form of Consciousness), resides not as much in the past or in distant origins, but more greatly so in the future toward which all things are drawn. In this light, the "Almighty God" (an optimal form of Greater Consciousness) awaits us in the future, in a "place" (or a set of conditions) that may be likened unto or called "Heaven."

This "God, Sum of all Consciousness" exists, and yes, existed in a primal form, presumably, in the past. Exists, yes, alive and now "breathing" in the present. Yet residing, even presiding, much more resoundingly and magnificently in the future.

The future is the direction toward which time itself—as well as all events, beings, and things—is drawn. In *that* direction and with great "gravity" awaits the Ultimate, at the culmination of all that is.

Until that time, the actions (born of conscious thought) of individual beings have *some* effects upon the whole outcome and its course over time. This influence of conscious beings, which is sometimes considerable, is more clearly recognized and understood at the impetus of the time and locality of each individual existence. Accordingly, some benefit is naturally realized immediately and incrementally by individuals progressing or advancing themselves as well as by those around them.

The *collective* actions of beings have relatively more pronounced effects upon the course and duration of larger events. Well-reasoned thought and actions performed by conglomerations of conscious beings can more assuredly affect the course of events in a decidedly constructive direction.

However, poorly reasoned or malevolent actions typically have unfortunate consequences. Accordingly, the timeline toward which optimal ideals might be materialized may theoretically be shortened or alternately stymied, eternally delayed, or subverted altogether.

But any of these sub-attainment scenarios, although theoretically possible, are vastly unfavorable and are therefore antithetical. Generally, the presumption is toward a gradual, and then a more rapid amelioration of conditions, as they are impacted by the ever-growing volume and aptness of the expanding conscious element.

This constitutes an introductory summary of the theory of Zenithity, and the related precursory process to be described as The Mechanysis of Perfunction.

New Words and Other Grammatical Offenses

New Words and Phrases

Please note that some of the key concepts, which are briefly introduced here, will be further described and elaborated upon throughout this book. Some key topics will have an entire chapter devoted to them further along. Please, let us suffice with brief summaries initially.

Zenithity

(Pronounced zee-NITH-it-ee OR zen-ITH-uh-ee *The syllables are spoken quite quickly.*)

Zenithity is the inevitable culmination of the forwardly ascendant nature of universal Consciousness (of which humanity is a localized example). Zenithity represents the *ul-*

timate state of the flourishing of reality as it becomes increasingly dominated by the most highly evolved form(s) of Greater Consciousness. This state is validly perceived and described as "ultimate"— in a literal way and especially from the perspective of Life and Consciousness.

Likewise, the *process* along that path, once it has been clearly set and nearly irreversible, may also be called Zenithity. As such, the definition encompasses both a state and a process which are essentially the same from our current perspective. Because this *process*, at its advanced stage, is nearly indistinguishable from its own theoretical conclusion. Alternately, it can be perceived as a process that serves as a conclusion, or a conclusion that is in fact an ongoing yet reliable process (since once upon an infinite timeline there is no literal "conclusion"). This "latter-day" process occurs during a time in the future wherein the inevitable "conclusion" (an idealized attainable process orientation) has become consciously ascertained.

So, Zenithity may be seen as a process more than a destination, place, or a moment in time. It may be seen as a somewhat infinite process, or alternately as an endpoint *encompassing* an infinite process (just as the origin of time can be visualized in a similar and seemingly paradoxical manner). It perhaps extends beyond the alternate origin point known as "the absolute future." It can be seen as a tight, highly streamlined process at the advanced edge of the continuum of Consciousness.

Yet still, the process of Zenithity *does begin to occur* at some point in real time. It 'kicks in' progressively or materializes at some point due to momentum from various other random and consciously directed activities. It represents a focused drawing toward a rational, idealized culmination.

The word *Zenithity* was chosen to describe this theoretical process/state because the root word "zenith" denotes the period in which something is at its most powerful or successful, or at its peak of brilliance. The suffix "-ity" forms a type of noun that expresses the state, condition or quality of the root word. Thus, the word *Zenithity* is intended to describe a state of perpetual advancement into an ultimate or peak set of conditions.

During Zenithity, Consciousness and Life become dominant over Time and Space, and they exert an enlightened and empowered influence over the remaining course of events. The influence over the course of events may be seen as "enlightened" due to the continuous amelioration of the conscious element. Since Consciousness is selective, the ever-growing effect it exerts is according to the sum of its own net willful volitions. Due to the magnitude of the ongoing event of Zenithity, we are drawn toward it and to the future within which it is held.

This directional amelioration may eventually be considered "providential," especially in hindsight. Not in that the conclusion was defined, known, or ordained in its origin – for it was none of these things. Instead it will *seem* providential in that the nature of the fortunate conclusion, having been arrived at in a forwardly navigated manner by disparate elements of Consciousness, will be exceptional in its auspicious quality *far beyond* what could have been strictly formulated or planned.

The Mechanysis of Perfunction

Prior to the time when the process of Zenithity has been ascertained, another process will co-span, or intertwine with, another considerable period of time. This intermediate process, perhaps already beginning and continuing into the near future (yet prior to Zenithity) may be called "The Mechanysis of Perfunction."

In that process, and during that time span, Consciousness, and beings of higher consciousness will have begun to recognize the unmistakable effects of Life, indirectly and directly, upon the course of the universe via Futurology. Futurology, an interest in the future and in the possible outcomes to current actions, can be seen as the opposite or obverse of history, which is the study or understanding of the past.

During the Mechanysis of Perfunction, there will be a period of initial but diminishing uncertainty. Gradually a general cohesiveness and unity will evolve among conscious beings. Steered toward an awareness of The-All that resides more clearly in the future, their actions will steadily tend toward a Benevolent Truth—with immediate positive effects accrued incrementally and locally. However, there will be some division, some uncertainty, and some degree of rightful caution. If Wisdom prevails (and as it predictably should), Zenithity will be achieved. And if all is dashed, the Universe—and Life—might yet again be forced to reinvent itself.

Nonetheless, even if there is an infinity of potential reinventions, the rationality of Consciousness implies that these are not to be manifested. Instead, by the virtue of conscious prowess the process of Zenithity *will* eventually be realized in *this* manifestation of The-All. For this is the path that is most reasonable, most logical, and most auspicious.

Were there no consciousness whatsoever, this would not be true, but since Consciousness exists alongside Time and Space, this conceptual inevitability arises. Beyond what we can conceive, the way toward that which is ideal is *irresistible* to Consciousness, even though we do not yet know fully what constitutes the "ideal" or the best pathway toward those idealisms. Consciousness, in the meanwhile, will progressively meld space (and the matter within) across time, and will continue to evolve itself (as or becoming as Greater Consciousness).

The Awakening Dawn

The period of time that existed prior to the stirrings of higher sentiments and emotions (in the physical realms) may, in retrospect, be fairly called the Unconscious Eons. During these times, an underlying type of primordial consciousness stirred beneath the origins of the new and chaotic universe, erupting into forms and lifeforms alike. Yet even across those eons, chaos and form 'battled' time and again, but for a very long time, consciousness of the type that we know did not fully emerge or evolve. But somehow, after eons of semiconsciousness and chaos, Life—higher life—did finally emerge.

We are living, I believe, in the tail end of the Unconscious Eons, and therein we stand at a unique period of time within history. This period, "The Awakening Dawn," entails the very beginnings of consciousness recognizing its own bearing and impact upon the course of all events. Individually and collectively, humans begin to recognize more and more that they harbor not only the immense power to positively influence the outcomes of anything and everything, but they also become increasingly willing to shoulder the responsibility which comes with that knowledge.

The Awakening Dawn is an interesting time full of opportunity, uncertainty, and adventure. By the end of the period, we inevitably begin to see consciousness reflexively. Introspectively, we become more aware of the role and nature of consciousness. Our knowledge and awareness will grow geometrically, to the extent that we may effectively redefine the human species. This redefinition and refinement will occur repeatedly as we approach Zenithity. As seen in this light, a series of metamorphoses will occur as we emerge from the era of our awakening.

Our awareness of what is good and bad will likewise become enlightened as will our ability to more fully cultivate that which is beneficial. Slowly, this era will transition into a time wherein the awareness becomes comparatively heightened, and the associated behaviors and decisions become more confident, effective, and *appropriate*. The period that follows The Awakening Dawn (which perhaps in many ways overlaps with it) is characterized by the earliest stirrings of positive global directionality. During the transition between the Awakening Dawn and The Mechanysis of Perfunction, much of the work of establishing a direction and momentum toward Zenithity will be performed.

Timeline Drift

The exact timing of the timelines of these processes may have varied wildly (or may differ considerably in the future) among the different planets or spheres of Life within the Universe, but the general concepts and processes remain approximately the same—and conceptually they do most likely merge or convene universally at some point (as all positions might conceivably be swept into Zenithity, considering that pure consciousness may span any distance instantaneously and is perhaps not subject to light-speed limitations).

These four overlapping phases (relisted below) occur theoretically across *any* inhabited subsystem within *this* timespace continuum, which was created (knowingly or unknowingly) to serve these processes as they are drawn to the alternate origin point at the far future:

- The Unconscious Eons
- The Awakening Dawn
- The Mechanysis of Perfunction
- Zenithity

Note that these theoretical timelines are listed in order of traditional history, not in the obverse order as is favored by Futurology.

Consider also, that within a given sphere, a civilization with all its conscious beings might be extinguished before reaching the higher stages. This could occur due to a natural disaster or another calamity of a magnitude against which those fledgling beings were not yet advanced enough to avert, or could not persevere against. More likely, however, greater disasters of this sort would occur due to their own untenable self-destructive impulses, en masse.

Thus the timelines across the Universe do not necessarily need to be consistent or synchronized, but the *stages* across each individual subsystem will be roughly the same. Successes will come more quickly to some than to others. Some may fail completely.

It would be best, obviously, if the human planet—Earth—were more advanced than others, or at least if it were among those leading the pack. Or minimally, if it were at least *somewhere within* the leading pack, somewhere near the head of the class, or so we would hope. Shooting low, just being one of the surviving, remaining realms is the baseline minimal goal. (This perspective is, of course, from the ever so slightly biased viewpoint of an earth-bound human.)

Other New-ish Words, Phrases, and Capitalizations

Some of the phrases introduced in this book may or may not represent truly *new* topics or concepts. But the use of new wording can relieve us of a very staid or highly biased usage of an existing word or phrase. The exercise of using new words may be worthy on its own merits. It helps us break through the barriers of normal thought, since language is one of the primary vehicles of thought. Furthermore, using new words helps us look at existing concepts and thoughts in new and more creative ways. Perhaps by breaking free of the constraints of language we will be able to step outside of a jaded, half-awake understanding of certain ideas. Predetermined conclusions which predate and subjugate any act of conjecture or contemplation often reside squarely in the entrenched usage of overly familiar word-forms.

Most importantly, the act of "getting outside the box," may open us up to the idea that maybe, just maybe, there really can be "something new under the sun."

Greater Consciousness—This represents that aspect of reality that can be seen as the net sum of all consciousness, especially when including any form of consciousness that surpasses or exceeds our own individualized form of awareness. Since the absolute *evidence* of a God (or the lack of a God) does not clearly exist, Greater Consciousness can be seen as simply the net sum of all consciousness, whether that consciousness contains only biologically based beings or additionally contains theoretical forms of consciousness of any other conceivable types. Greater Consciousness can also be understood to include a more overarching 'godlike' form of primordial consciousness. Also, Greater Consciousness is, within this philosophy, considered to be most likely greater in magnitude, cohesiveness, depth, and scale in the distant Future than it is currently or than it has been at any point in the past.

The-All. In simplest terms, this can be defined as "all that is greater than oneself." Subjectively speaking, this becomes "all which *appears* greater than the self, yet including the self." In more objective terms, The-All is the Universe along with the Greater Consciousness that is intertwined or overlaid upon the physical reality of space-time. As such, this term could be used as an alternative to "the universe" (for the universe *can* be seen as encompassing all of consciousness, even though that term often indicates space-time *without* consciousness), as Greater Consciousness (for Greater Consciousness *can* be seen as fully encompassing the universe), or as God (for the term "God" has been used to describe either of these concepts in prior usage and sometimes to encompass all conscious beings).

While the term "universe" could be used interchangeably with "The-All," many would perceive "the universe" as meaning the vast realms of space populated with rocks, stars, and planets but somehow devoid of consciousness. The-All could be used interchangeably with the notion of God as an all-encompassing force, but when the word "God" is used, many people might draw up alternate images with either positive or negative connotations—connotations that are typically more limiting when compared with this term. Greater Consciousness, in a highly nuanced way, can be seen as including everything, but it is *more* accurate to envision The-All as containing both the physical universe *and* Greater Consciousness. In this paradigm we might consider the physical universe as an extension or construct of Greater Consciousness. In this way The-All can be visualized as *'the living universe'*.

Vigil-Mind. This term refers to a practical state of mind in which an individual commonly or quite frequently uses a combination of highly evolved mindsets. Fundamental to Vigil-Mind is an active application of reason and comparative logic. In this state, individuals engage in a well-reasoned and open-minded assessment of every situation and condition in which they are involved. It is a state wherein a degree of Zen-like mindfulness or awareness is coupled with a rational, skeptical, and analytical oversight. Ideally, the creative side of awareness is also freely expressed or is, at the very least, free to operate. It is a state wherein one may see beyond ordinary personal constraints or limiting societal influences. Hopefully, this state, involving combined types of forward-thinking mindsets, will allow us to make the utmost of every situation. Among these many attributes of Vigil-Mind are; a keen awareness, the clarity of careful and well-thought reason, and an adventurous and fun-loving sense of creativity.

All aspects of Vigil-Mind already exist and are already used from time to time by many people. Thinking that includes wide-eyed awareness, intentional clarity of reason, and adventurous and frivolous creativity has led to most of humanity's advancements in the last five hundred years.

The main thing really new about the term "Vigil-Mind" is the assertion that the rate of occurrence of this mode of thinking will increase rather dramatically in the immediate future—in our lifetimes. This increase, along with the application of Vigil-Mind and the study of Futurology, will most likely lead to *newer* modes of advanced thinking, heretofore unimagined. Arising from the application of Vigil-Mind and the study of Futurology, entirely new ways of thinking will emerge. This is the primary novelty regarding the term "Vigil-Mind"; that this mode of thinking, available to us now, eventually transmutes and thereby helps usher in newer forms of awareness. These greater forms of awareness become increasingly instrumental during the Mechanysis of Perfunction.

So, for now, the concept of Vigil-Mind implies a situation in which these existing modes of advanced thinking become "a thing" and begin to occur much more commonly and effortlessly.

Atypical Capitalizations. Do not be alarmed when encountering words which are capitalized in a manner that is not entirely normal.

"What? Impossible. Oh, my."

Yes. Just as a few new words are employed as needed, some words are newly capitalized in a non-standard manner. Words representing something of a higher or greater nature, anything exalted or sublime, these may be capitalized in some but not all instances—depending upon the usage or *context*. The idea is to broaden our palate and appreciation for the usage of certain words representing those qualities, concepts, entities, or essences which might truly *deserve* capitalization. Perhaps this practice can, at least minimally, serve to elicit our awareness and potentially elevate our consideration accordingly.

For example, the word "life" can be better distinguished when capitalized in some usages. A lower case is used in statements like "he lived a good life." Whereas the same word may deserve an uppercase rendering in sentences like "we belong to the grand realm of Life." Or we can consider the description of life as a mere biological function as deserving of a lower-case rendering, as in, "there were no signs of life in the stagnant pond." But we might consider capitalization in sentences like, "we cherish Life, above all."

Since it might be annoying to invent *too many* new words, existing words must suffice in many use cases. This becomes especially true when observing contextual capitalizations which prompt us to consider slightly elevated variations of certain existing words.

Simply because this approach to capitalization is used in *some* instances does not mean that failing to do so in all instances is wrong. Hopefully this practice is simple enough to appreciate and should cause no undue confusion or frustration for the reader. It simply means that I, as an author, felt that adding the emphasis of capitalization to certain words, in certain contexts, seemed appropriate, of some merit, and hopefully has added some value.

Non-Standard Usage of Ordinary Words

In addition to introducing a few rather new-ish words (as described in the sections above), there are some existing words that will be used in some slightly non-standard ways. The usage of these words might involve introducing or favoring a nuanced new meaning to an existing word. In other cases, a word's meaning in this book might represent a word's older meaning or perhaps its original meaning. This may need to occur when the modern day meaning of certain words has morphed considerably and those words have acquired considerable nuanced "baggage" layered upon the original, often much purer, meaning.

Evolve. To avoid issues of semantics, please be aware that the term "evolve" is not necessarily used here in its strictly scientific context. For most of us, the nuance of this usage will be obvious since the term "evolve" has itself evolved. Statements herein regarding evolution do not refer directly to the word's meaning under Darwinism. Used here, it implies a more intentional, progressive, conscious-driven notion of evolution of both physical beings and of Consciousness in general. Environmental scientists would most likely cringe at the notion that evolution implies "progress." Moreover, they would likely embrace beliefs that ascribe changes in species or systems over time to totally *random* reactions to other equally random changes in the environment of a species or the broader environment of a system. Used here, the word "evolve" *does* imply a notion of progress (see below) and, when used in the future (in this book), it will quite often imply that same *progressive* meaning.

Progress - To leave no room for ambiguity, let's clarify that "progress" is used to mean the accomplishment or development of more positive and beneficial changes over time. As such, the opposite of progress is regression. While it may seem odd that a word as simple as "progress" needs clarification, it does. Why? Because in writing we are trying to convey certain discrete concepts while using a language that is sometimes laden with multilayered veils of subtle inference. In short, there are some, whose minds are so influenced by politically nuanced overtones, that they can only associate "progress" with "progressives," a term which *they* believe is only associated with liberals, socialists, or communists.

We (that is the normal rational thinking folk) are 'taking back' the word "progress" from fringe groups (on *either* side of the political spectrum) and away from politically biased overtones. Let us wipe clean any politicized overtones that we have attached to the word (and concept) of *progress*. Within these pages, the word "progress" will mean *actual* progress in the more traditional meaning of the word, or more specifically, the act of making something genuinely better (whatever that may entail). Progress is basically amelioration, but the word "progress" is so much easier to use and better known.

To take it a step further, can we check our politically and religiously charged definitions and colorations of all words in general? At least for the remainder of the reading of this book, please?

So, in summary, "evolve" will be used in an enhanced or expanded manner, while "progress" will be used in a more fundamental or traditional way—the way the word was originally intended to be used.

I believe we can all manage to understand the meanings implied, regardless of the wording or capitalizations used.

And isn't the underlying meaning what really matters?

So, concerning words, enough said!

Next, let's take a journey through space and time!

Actually, you literally take a journey through space and time every time you walk down the street.

Hmmm...

So, maybe this time let's just take a journey through the *concepts* of time and space. More importantly, let's explore our *perceptual understandings* of space and time. And that's a journey we *don't* take every day.

The Way to the Present

We might visualize or graphically represent *space* as a simple dot moving across a line called *time*. The dot represents the current position (and condition) of space in the present. Usually, the future is depicted on the right side of a theoretically infinite line, while the past is portrayed as the leftmost portion of that presumed infinitely long line. The present and where we are now is displayed as a single "dot" right smack in the middle. It is ironic, almost to the point of being humorous, that the vast infinity of space, along with everything in it, is represented as a single, tiny dot. A greater oversimplification has never existed!

But let's continue with this commonly used, albeit overly simplistic, model.

What is behind the dot (and depicted on its left) is the past, which is represented by the portion of the line that consists of all the previous positions and conditions of "space" (the dot), during all the moments that occurred *prior to* reaching the current position and state of the dot (the present). To fully visualize this, imagine a series of dots extending *into infinity* along the line to the left of and leading up to, the "present dot." (This will be illustrated in Image #1)

The future is then typically represented by all of those potential moments (positions and conditions of space) that will occur *after* the current position of the dot (i.e., after the present). Notably, this future portion of the line lies in the direction *toward which the dot is moving.* The future, within this simple model, is an unbounded number of theoretical future "dots"—all lined up on the right-hand side of the "present dot."

Image #1 - Past, Present*, and Future as Dots along an Infinite Timeline

(*The present is the rather special dot shown in the middle.)

While it is perhaps a most dramatic oversimplification, this graphical conceptualization is still somewhat useful. Before proceeding, though, let us not forget, that the "dot" covers an infinitely large amount of *space* in every direction (it represents all of 3-dimensional space)—encompassing everything in the known and unknown universe as well as the current conditions *of* all those physical entities occupying *all* of space. Furthermore, let us not be deceived by a short line drawn on a piece of paper. For the timeline itself, which is *also* infinite, represents a different form of infinity in that it is strictly linear. We could say that time is limitless but only in a linear direction. But it could be *more* accurate to state that the timeline is linearly infinite in *two* directions; past and future. As an aside, since the timeline is eternal in both directions, the infinitely sized volume of space (the dot) is *not really* in the middle—since theoretically, there is no "middle" of an infinitely long line.

So, we can use this model to begin to see a clearer and much larger representation of the traditional "space-time continuum": an unimaginably large dot having infinite *spatial* dimensions (filled with an unlimited array of "things" like stars, planets, rocks, people, etc.), moving across a "line" that likewise has infinitely large *spatial* dimensions to accommodate the infinitely large "dot." Events, actions, and interactions, occur across the timeline among the many "things" and "beings" which occupy space, but they occur *only* with the motion of the dot across the timeline in the forward direction. Every event and interaction that occurs within the dot, "that infinite space filled with infinite things", occurs only *when* or *as* the "dot" advances across the timeline. Whether at the molecular level, the universal level, or anywhere in between, *nothing* happens if the dot does not roll along. If the dot were somehow not moving, there would be no actions, events, or motions of any type—because those only occur when there is a change in time. Without time, there can be no change, and everything would remain in a rigid 'frozen' state.

Clearly, this simplified line of time has a distinct past (capable of containing an immeasurable, linear number of limitlessly enormous sized spatial dots) and a *potential* future with a likewise infinite number of linear "places" or "positions" capable of holding an ever-changing "present" of similarly immeasurable spatial size.

It is important to note that the only "real" dot depicted on the line is the one representing the present. The line extending *toward* the dot from the past, and the line extending *away* from the dot into the future, can be seen more as a "tunnel" with spatial dimensions large enough to encompass the entire physical universe. As such, the past and future portions of the line are not composed of dots, but rather are a more fluid succession of "positions" along the massive, tubelike timeline. (However, we may continue to use dots on some of the drawings to help demonstrate the whole of space passing through the "tunnel" of time.)

And while it may seem obvious, it is worth mentioning that there is an absolute directionality attributed to the timeline—the "dot" (the immense spatial present) is *always* moving away from the past and into the present (or the next, newest present), before edging ever onward into the future. This is to say, the dot has already occupied every position along the linear tunnel coming from the past, but it has not yet occupied any portion of the linear "tube" extending into the future.

As we flesh out the narrative, the meaning of the simple drawing becomes much clearer, no?

But can we tweak this simple model further to more closely express the nature of reality?

Well, it seems rather apparent that there *was* a very distinct linear past (or a path if you will) that was taken to arrive at this present moment. And from the moment just before the now, the living and very real present dissipates entirely.

This moment, the present, is constantly "stolen" by the past.

It seems that *this* current moment is constantly pulled *from* the immediate future. It then immediately becomes the reality of the present moment during which *all* events occur. And then, that moment is just as instantly *given over* to the past. The present is always dropping away, eroding, or fading instantly into the past, while it is simultaneously being fed by and reinvigorated by the future.

Even as the present moment is forever stolen by the past, it is always "hungry" and forever eating away into the future. The present is never lost, nor does it increase or decrease, for what it loses to the past it always regains from the future.

But, once the moment has moved into the past, that moment no longer really exists. Forever inflexible its shell remains. It seems that it becomes thereafter locked into whatever state it was in at that time when it 'was' the present. But even that is a fantasy, for as it immediately fades it becomes a rigidly cast memory *at best*. While a fragment of a past moment may exist in our memories, the moment itself does not really exist at all anymore. When it is gone, it's gone. The instant the present inches forward, the previous iteration of itself is gone—along with all the countless former iterations of "the present."

But if we could somehow magically review any one of those past moments, we would find that it has been fixed, as if set in stone. The entire progression of past moments represents an inflexible, static, linear progression of all conditions across all objects (and beings). The absolute knowledge of everything within all of those expired past moments would constitute an absolute and complete literal history of everything. Of course, none of us can possibly possess awareness of that volume and level of detail. Nor can we expect to derive the exact history of everything from artifacts, clues, traces, and relics existing solely in the present.

But the future 'moment', that piece of time that always awaits just ahead in the future, is not rigid at all; instead, it is filled with possibility and potential. Unlocked, it has not yet been 'written in stone' or 'locked' in any way. However, as the immediate future passes through the present, it is acted upon. Then it loses all of its flexibility, and it becomes a permanent 'shell-like' fixture immediately as it moves into the past. Never again does *that* moment live or change.

Gigantic in scope and scale, beyond comprehension, is each and every iteration of the spatial "dot" that travels through time. At each moment, that spatial dot is clearly vast in terms of space and everything within space. So, the past contains a linear succession of such infinitely sized "dots" or positions, which form a "tubelike" history that accommodates such dots in a seamlessly fluid progression. Bear in mind, that the historical dots may be 'theoretical' or simply remembrances whereas the present dot – wherein change is occurring presently – is very real.

But for all we know, the tubelike "linear" path of the past might be quite jagged, curved, or random in shape and appearance. We have no means by which to know whether this path of successive iterative states of change to the historical spatial dots forms a *straight* line or not. We only know that the events occurred in a succession—one after the other.

The actual "line," while continuous, may have been curved, crooked, zig-zagged, or most likely just randomly shaped. Regardless of shape, it clearly consists of a rather fixed iterative succession of the spatial dots. One exact set of conditions across the infinity of *spatial* dots led to the next exact set of conditions across that infinity. This changing of conditions across *everything* within space has continued, unbroken in this manner, throughout historical time up until the present. Each iteration of space (the present), representing change, is perhaps a millionth of a millisecond in length of time. Or, perhaps more likely, it is indivisible and truly fluid (in terms of linear time).

To reiterate, in the past there has clearly been a "linearlike" succession relating the exact set of conditions and positions of *everything* within the spatial dot, from one moment to the next. And it was necessary to proceed through that exact procession of change within the series of spatial dots, in order to arrive *exactly* at the current set of infinite spatial conditions that now constitute the present.

Stated differently, the present is an ever-fleeting moment in which everything, every incalculable thing, is an exact 'way,' or an exact set of conditions and positions. At least this is true at the *very instant* the moment passes forever into the past. That exact set of conditions and positions of everything is (seemingly) the derivative sum of all the previous linear positions of "past presents," having occurred continuously in a strictly sequential order.

Yet in the same instance, just before the moment moves into the past, *this* present "moment" is rather fluid. Perhaps the present can be seen as having an immeasurably small size in the direction of time. In other words, the present "dot" is most likely not "digital" or divisible down to a particular size. The moment is not "divisible" or quantizable—or at least it does not seem to have those characteristics. It appears that the "present moment" consists of an *infinitely large* segment of three-dimensional space, occupying an *infinitely small* yet fluid slice of time within which all events occur.

The present is that mixing pot within which all change occurs.

For after change occurs, all previous segments of time become set or fixed, in that they can never again be changed. No longer of much consequence, they now constitute an intricately complex history that no one can fathom. They can never be truly "relived" again, so that eternal string of past "presents" can never be accessed again except via our memories or recordings of those events (or perhaps via the memories of Greater Consciousness).

In their own times, the past "presents" in this infinite string were of massive importance. And they still are important is some ways, but *primarily* because their importance echoes forward into the present. Their key significance is that they have determined the exact nature of the *all-important present* in which we now reside. Thus, each moment is born of the exact succession of the entire prior progression of linear moments. Conversely, the current moment, just as it begins to arise, would not be as it is now if it were not for that exact progression of previous (spatially infinite) moments.

Incredible. All of this is quite incredible. Clearly, this is beyond our reach to fully comprehend, yet it is amazing that in our minds we can even partially conceive of any of this at all. But we can. So, we realize that it is possible for us to imagine and model these things in simple form, and all of these conceptualizations regarding reality surely seem reasonable or plausible. Otherwise, we would immediately modify or discard them.

It is only if *all* of reason is unreliable that these notions are not representative of reality—at least in some measure. But if reason is entirely broken, then we might exist in a reality wherein we have no hope of comprehending anything in any way. If all of reason is broken and unreliable, then all of our notions about everything, including our science, are likewise broken.

These models, related to time and space, are in fact reasonable simplifications; and reason, although fallible, is typically reliable. Despite any flaws inherent within reason, it remains the primary tool we have at our disposal for understanding the underlying nature of this type of phenomenon. So, while reason is fallible, we must conclude that it is *generally* reliable; since it is, we may continue with our fair conjecture and analysis.

This exercise is primarily to take an overview of time: past, present, and future and to become more fully aware of what it is, and of our place within that timeline. Most importantly, these summaries can expand our ideas about the nature of the reality in which we live.

As always, some will argue against one detail or another.

For example, the science buff may argue that space is not *truly* infinite according to some of the newer theories of astrophysics. But if space is not infinite, then what lies outside the boundaries of that space? Obviously, *something* theoretically does, and that "something" can only be *more space*.

Perhaps we are speaking of two different entities when we refer to space. The modern physicist now uses the term "space" to refer to some newly discovered invisible "substance" that *seems* to fill the empty portions of the known universe. On the other hand, I am referring, in a more traditional manner, to the infinity of actual *empty space* which conceptually holds everything—bounding everything yet unbounded. Empty space inherently bounds, exceeds, and contains, *everything*. Everything, by definition, exists within the confines of absolute space; everything includes the newly defined "space" of the more substantial format described by the modern physicist. The warped concept of space is itself bounded by an infinity of traditional "empty" space.

There probably should have been two words describing these two very different notions of 'space' – and while both may be very real, they are both very different. But when they (scientists) discovered this underlying "force" that fills much of what we formerly thought of as empty "space," they began redefining "space" as being *only that* thing (the mysterious force that fills part of space). Their hijacking of the word "space" means there are now two meanings; this inadvertently created some confusion that requires this brief disambiguation. They forgot that the other type of space, truly *empty* space, still extends eternally and still encompasses the other "substance" which has been improperly defined or described as "space." A better term for the newer concept of space might be "space substance," instead of just "space," since the concept (and reality) of space is that of a preexisting (yet empty) entity. It is a term that traditionally describes the infinitely sized 'box' of emptiness within which *everything* exists.

And concerning arguments over details, others might contend (after watching too many sci-fi movies), that time travel (or going backward in time) is possible just because some scientist determined via math that some particles could have a behavior and a property of *seeming* to go ever so fractionally backward in time. At this point, we do not wish to split hairs over nuanced scientific findings. Instead, we are considering the *general* nature of our conscious reality in which we find ourselves. This is the meta-reality in which Life exists—not the realm of particle physics in which particles exist. The point is, you are not a particle, and *time* does not travel backward, and *you* will never travel back in time—only forward.

So, let's get off the fantasy 'high horse', for it is really a rather childlike 'hobby horse'. Even if we would like to believe in a fantasy that *seems* to be driven by science, the truth is apparent and undeniable: time moves from the past, through the present, and into the future. It does not operate in reverse. We are never going back in time. The universe is not going retrograde, it is moving steadily, incrementally, and fluidly via the present into the future.

The spatial universe, in which we are embedded,
travels forever forward in time,
always plunging ever more deeply into the future.

Anyway, we could go on and on, refuting various 'arguments' or calming the anxieties of those whose feathers were ruffled by our somewhat direct conclusions. But we are not looking for arguments. Instead we are *philosophically* seeking relevant and rational explanations that define and support our place as conscious entities within the greater cosmos. Is that OK?

A little patience is needed at this juncture, for we are looking first at space and time from a conscious rational perspective before looking more directly at consciousness itself.

So, in continuation…

Nuanced scientific (or fantastical) discussions aside, the primary points we have covered are *nearly* irrefutable, or at least they possess a *level of validity* that is difficult to step away from entirely. Primarily, these points are, that there is an infinitely sized "space-dot" (fluidly containing everything) which has traveled down an eternally linear set (from our perspective) of past iterations to reach the present. That is a premise that is hard to dodge. But the next part is open to a little more interpretation, as it should be, for it refers to the future.

An Eye to the Future

Since the past has neatly consisted of a linear succession of "presents"—albeit a potentially jagged succession of linear presents—to arrive at *this* present, we often conclude that the timeline moving into the future is likewise strictly linear. We draw a line with an arrow facing to the left to represent an infinite past. Then in the middle of the line, we draw a dot representing the infinity of static (yet somehow momentarily changing) conditions that constitute the present. Then we draw a right-facing arrow at the end of the line extending to the right of the "present dot". This forward-pointing or right-seeking line represents, in simplest terms, the infinity of a linear future.

Image #2—Simple Classic Linear Timeline

(Infinite past to the left, infinite future to the right, present as dot)

But simply because a very linear and true historical path of successive presents occurred to lead us to the now, does this mean that the future too is strictly linear? Certainly, after it has become past, it is linear (or at least sequential); but then it is past, and it is part of a set progression of occurrences that are (or were) quite rigid (from our perspective now). But until (or before) the future occurs, is it linear?

Perhaps it is best to perceive the future as essentially "fanning out" into a series of possible directions or differing sets of conditions—somewhat like a probability cloud but more like a fan-shaped structure of possibilities extending into the future. Certainly, the trajectory or momentum of the present, as conducted by the past, might preclude some possible futures in the immediate sense. But from a larger perspective, and considering that the future "timeline" is infinite in the forward direction, we could say that an infinite array of possible future timelines fans out from the present.

Image #3—Forward Direction, Rigid Past, Fanlike Future

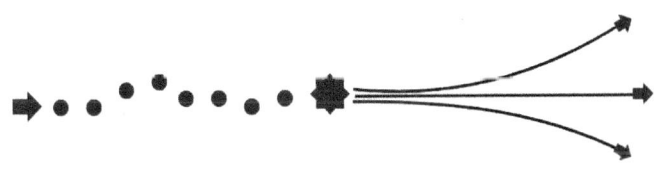

(Illustrates proper forward directionality of past. Past flexibility, now rigid. Illustrates broad fan-like flexibility of the future.)

This set of possible futures represents a stacked series of countless potential timelines, resulting in future "present" states that consist of every imaginable set of conditions available to any given future "present." While ostensibly infinite, the set of future conditions is, in the immediate sense, reduced somewhat by the *current state* of the present and its 'trajectory' or momentum. Nonetheless, while the set of infinite future possibilities is (temporarily) reduced by that portion unreachable due to the immediate momentum (present state as projected by the past), it is still an incalculably infinite set of possibilities.

And for the whole universal system this diagram is generally representative (or true), but it also scales down to a more localized *version* of truth regarding possibility for the individual. For while the momentum of our past circumstances (leading into the real state of the present) might make *some* conclusions immediately less likely than others, the future remains open-ended regarding our potential actions and the transitory conditions surrounding us.

Now, some would argue that the trajectory of future events is set in motion strictly from the past. Extending through the present, that presumption predicts an irrefutable future timeline that is rigid or unyielding. Proponents of this argument would contend that *all* things continue and will resolve in a rigid linear fashion. This is perhaps the basis behind ideas of predestination or preordination. And if those ideas are true, then nothing we do matters—for in that paradigm, we will do all that we do simply because we too will have been predestined to do them. If that presumption is true, for example, then I am writing all of this because I was "predestined" to do so, even though I am questioning predestination as a part of a presumably predestined action. This is ironic at best.

Perhaps the universe has a sense of humor after all.

We may find the comfortable notion of predeterminism very tempting. After all, wouldn't it be nice to have a built-in excuse or alibi for every misstep and misdemeanor? And since this notion relies upon solely circular logic, it is nearly impossible to disprove.

However, we can certainly argue against predestination—and we will. And of course, those who argue in favor of predestination will simply say that our arguments against it were themselves predestined to be. And there again, we see how the proponents of predestination theories have set up a circular, self-fulfilling prophecy, and perhaps nothing more.

In refutation of the notion of a rigid, linear, predestined timeline, we again merely need to apply the attribute of reason. For it is difficult to ignore, at least in our individual lives, the clear effects of our own actions as they affect outcomes in the immediate future. So, that leads us to a conclusion in which we, via our actions, may cause a differing set of futures to occur—even if the difference in outcomes seems very small or insignificant (on a universal scale).

If any action by any conscious being can bring about a different resulting set of conditions, even if it affects the entire set of universal conditions in only one tiny way, then *that* consciously influenced set of conditions is not *exactly* the same as the set of conditions that would have occurred if the conscious being had taken no action (or perhaps had taken a different action).

This "common knowledge" that there *is* cause and effect can be overlooked or dismissed generally as being overtly obvious, but not in a discussion of predeterminism, and in that discussion especially when the principle of 'cause and effect' applies to actions committed by conscious entities (like humans). If a conscious action can and does cause a different set of conditions to emerge or unfold, then the future contains inherently at least more than one linear "option." In fact, since conscious beings existing in the trillions across the universe can affect "gazillions" of small conditions in each moment, there can be said to exist an infinity of potentially differing linear futures, comprising potentially every combination of outcomes conceivable—and inconceivable.

The conscious altering of conditions and outcomes occurs *outside* of a rigidly predetermined set of events ordered by the weight of the vast momentum of the past, in that the momentum of the past, while significant, **is not inescapable in the long run.**

Hence, in our elemental 'stick drawings' the fanlike pattern more clearly represents the future than does a strictly linear "line." But we eventually must depart from our simple line art, for the fanlike pattern eventually forms an ever outwardly curving pattern, such that it has the potential to include any *possible* future timeline. As such, this notion is not easily represented by primitive 'drawings'. Furthermore, it was never intended that the line drawings would be uber-realistic, but instead, they are meant to assist us in discussing or visualizing some of these concepts which are admittedly so difficult to fully behold.

Take a Deep Breath

Let's relax, if we may, and keep it all in perspective.

Bear in mind, that all of this is merely an exercise. It is an exercise that would have us reflect upon the nature of time and space, and upon the relationships between past, present, and future.

In this exercise, most critically, we now begin to focus upon the location, role, condition, and impact of *conscious beings*, both within and upon the timeline.

In the perpetual timeline, it seems that we as conscious beings can and do continuously act upon conditions within the present and we do so in willful anticipation of the future.

And while all the other points may be debatable, and much of it may be of little or no relevance whatsoever, *this* understanding is highly significant:

Conscious beings perpetually affect the timeline itself,
by successively and persistently allocating preferable future
conditions and events
via their actions in the mutable present.

Some of these more "preferable" conditions are physical, and they constitute very real changes within the physical world. Examples include farming for food, constructing a simple building, diverting population from a hurricane due to satellite weather warnings, or shooting a missile to redirect an oncoming meteor. Each of these types of actions alters the set of *all* conditions along the future timeline in a very real and physical sense, regardless of how small the effect may appear from our own localized perspectives (or from a more universal perspective). And we must remember that there are trillions of such actions occurring across the universe within each moment.

While many of the preferable conditions implemented by consciousness are physical, some of these more preferable conditions are enacted *internally*. As such, the conscious selection of successively more preferable internal conditions can represent enhancements or elevations to the state of the conscious beings themselves.

Some internal enhancements, achieved by conscious beings across many vectors, incrementally enable those beings to become even more effective at selecting and implementing preferable future conditions, on an ever-growing scope and scale.

The effects can thus be geometrically cumulative, with a potentially cascading effect.

Consciousness itself will reign over the future,
ever favoring the preferable;
unrelentingly elevating conditions,
both externally and internally.

The Missing Link

The present is the melting pot of change. Therein *all* change occurs.

The forces leading up to the present influence it via the vast momentum of the previous moment, and that moment was influenced by the vast momentum of every other previous linear moment. But despite the great influence of the past upon the present, something else exerts an influence within the present: *consciousness*. Life exerts its ever-growing influence upon the present as it assesses, judges, and *acts upon*, all things.

**As such, Life, even if only casually,
makes not only a causal impact, but also a willful impact.**

Life not only influences the present, in which it *always* resides, but via impacting the present, it also impacts the future "timeline" as well. Life, whether knowingly or unknowingly, exerts some degree of influence (especially in its immediate spatial vicinity) upon the present, and thereby 'diverts' or 'redirects' the future. Life affects the set of conditions in the present, and by extension influences the selection of future sets of conditions.

Life, in some measure, selects the future.
As consciousness grows, Life, more and more,
begins to influence the future in intentional ways.

For, to the living, the logic is as follows: "I inhabit the present, and it exists in a set of conditions. I wish to modify this set of conditions, in the present, so that I may be safer, happier, and more content in this present."

As we grow wiser and more capable, that logic extends: "I know that in the future, I will exist in a series of future-present states. In those future sequences of "presents" I would like some of the specific conditions to be different from—strike that—*better than* the set of conditions in my current present reality. Ideally, I want my future set of conditions to be *better* than every past series of very underwhelming experiences or conditions with which I had to contend."

This is powerful stuff, and it is directly observable, and achievable, by the individual. Is this not clear? By being observable, *our own influence, within our own sphere of existence,* is in fact empirically and thus 'scientifically' knowable and 'known.' That one's conscious actions can create a deliberate change in future conditions is a fundamentally known and factually irrefutable aspect of reality. It is not theoretical, it is real. The changes that occur are not always exactly as the protagonist had intended, but the cause-and-effect nature of reality is clearly observable, especially regarding the impacts of the actions of thought-driven lifeforms. One's own consciousness, as a causative factor, can be easily demonstrated in its immediate and very real effects.

Consciousness, by exerting itself, can and does elicit an effect. Consciousness is thus a '*cause*' *or a causative factor.* And that which we can affect and observe within the individual sphere is much more magnified within the plural form of the statement; "*We* want this set of conditions to be different in the future series of events." (FYI, "*we*" is the keyword in that sentence.)

Powerful though this is at the human societal level, there are conceivably numerous different forms of consciousness within the universe, and perhaps even *pervading* the universe in different sectors or across differing levels. Some would go so far as to say that consciousness created the universe, or at the very least, that consciousness is as fundamental as time and space. The density with which consciously animated physical beings populate the universe is unknown (to us), but even if only our one world exists, that one world alone, filled with consciously evolving beings is *highly significant.*

It stands to reason that there are most likely countless other civilizations consisting of consciously animated physical beings throughout the Universe. And beyond these physically based "corporeal" forms of conscious beings, there *may* be other forms of "higher" consciousness that may be, from our perspective, more or less incorporeal from our perspective – or—instead—somewhat energy-based forms of consciousness.

If any of these alternate forms exist, their type of consciousness may determine their level and type of awareness. Accordingly, their consciousness may determine the types of actions that the conscious entity can take upon various aspects of reality—matter, space, time, or upon itself, a form of consciousness.

Consciousness, whether it is a newly emerged 'by-product' of space-time (and matter), or an originating element predating the continuum, is now a significant or co-equivalent "partner" in the time-space continuum. This may be a sorely 'missing link' regarding modern science – for they neither attribute any role nor any bearing to Consciousness.

In truth, Consciousness is the greater of the forces,
and, at least from our own perspective, the most important.

Consciousness has a vested interest in the present—for it resides therein—all across the infinity of the Universe. Consciousness fills the "space-dot" on our imaginary timeline just as much as does matter. And as the space-dot passes through time, (and if there were no consciousness involved), then all the matter within the dot and *everything physical* would change in a very passive manner—*as if* via some form of random blind predestination. But consciousness *does* exist. And consciousness acts willfully in the present, and its actions have clear and dramatic effects upon matter and upon the very course of future events across time. So the notion of "predestination" or of a hapless, aimless, hurtling of spatial events through time is replaced *to some extent* by a notion of **conscious "steerage."** (This becomes more predominant as we approach Zenithity.)

While the effect of conscious change to the physical realm grows, more astonishingly, we come to recognize that Consciousness can also change *itself*. It grows, mutates, evolves, improves, expands. And thereby its effects upon hard matter can be further compounded—geometrically, at times.

And of course this would be so, for Consciousness has a perspective and acts with feeling—for the vessel of the present (and all future "presents") is its home. We live and reside, in the fluid present, and through projection, into the future. Consciousness does not just reside passively in the space of the present like so many dead rocks or meteors floating aimlessly in a void. Consciousness resides in the realm of space (or perhaps in a different "conscious space") in an active, deliberate, and very engaging manner of awareness.

Here is another allegory: Consciousness acts upon reality, upon the present and the future, in a very aware and willful manner. So, the effects of consciousness are not like so many billiard balls scattered randomly upon their "breaking." Pedantically, a physicist might contend, that the motion and velocity of every billiard ball can be calculated from that apparently random "breaking up" of the whole pile of them; thus, their dispersal is not, in fact, *random*.

To that I might answer, "I will wholeheartedly agree that those forces upon billiard balls *could* be calculated, even though I *know* that neither *you* nor anyone else will never perform that actual calculation on this particular breaking of the balls."

But, more critically, the 'calculability' observation is totally off skew from the point, which is:

Consciousness, while exerting a highly significant influence, is NOT predictable by the rather dumb laws of physics. Neither is the influence of consciousness random. Nor is its influence predictable, bounded, controlled, or limited in any way.

So, considering the unique role of this fundamental property that we call "consciousness," we might consider a new "dimension" in our study of physics. To our "scientific" understandings of the universe, it may be best to consider an expanded continuum that includes Consciousness: The Time-Space-Consciousness continuum. For regardless of its *original* status within this triad (which is unknown), it has become, and increasingly will become, a "more than co-equal partner" as we move into the future.

Consciousness, by having been sorely omitted from the equation and from science in general, has become another "missing link." Another cosmic irony is that the greatest realm awaiting scientific exploration and discovery is this missing link, which obviously has been right beneath our noses all this time. (Or at least somewhere in that vicinity.)

Consciously Independent Conclusions

As a conscious being, you may certainly draw your own conclusions about all of this.

That's the way it is, and the way it is "supposed" to be.

From my perspective, this is a really, really, good thing.

To draw one's own conclusions, and to act upon them, is the literal embodiment of the notion that conscious beings can willfully consider and then effectuate matters independently.

And this fact further asserts the previously stated ideas about the independence of the conscious influence.

Thank you for not being a dumb billiard ball!

Consciousness: The Third Dimension

Consciousness, as we experience it, is tied to space and time. We are forever bound to the present, while having remembrance, hopefully fond, of the past and at best learning from it. And from our vantage point in the present, we even have some foresight or anticipation regarding the future. But to be clear, we exist solely in the present, and in that habitat do we solely reside.

Yet it is not too difficult to imagine that a form of consciousness is perhaps the only phenomenon that could possibly exist *outside* of space and time. Matter clearly can't exist outside of space, and it can't exist outside of time (the atomic particles making all matter require constant motion, which requires time). But one can nearly imagine a form of consciousness that *could* exist outside of time, and outside of space. And as such, that form of consciousness *could* have predated time and space, and perhaps *could* have spawned time and space. And as unlikely as this sounds, the spontaneous (non-conscious) arising of time, space, and all matter within the universe seems even *more* unlikely.

The idea of a consciously emanated universe is sheer speculation of course, because none of us has experienced that *type* of consciousness—the type that could manifest by volition all of space, time, and matter into existence.

Imagination—what a strange commodity indeed. It gives us the capacity to speculate, without which we would be like reactive robots, or even worse, dumb billiard balls.

Aside from considering an imaginary form of consciousness as potentially external to the space-time continuum, doesn't it seem like *something* is missing from the 'continuum' when it is described in merely those two parts? If we say, "here is empty space" and then we say, "there is time ticking across the emptiness of space," is it not clear that *something* is missing? The elephant in the room is consciousness. Without consciousness the space-time continuum would be a stupid and empty thing.

This is somewhat like the old riddle of Eastern lore which asks, "If a tree falls in the forest but no one is around, does it make a sound?"

There are many ways to approach this riddle, but it can be summed up as this: If no one is there, there is no ear to hear, and thus no sound as we define it. The deeper (implied) question is, without an observer isn't any scene void and empty? If there is no observer—no consciousness—isn't all of matter just a void of clutter and nonsense? Isn't it all emptiness and pointlessness, without Life, without consciousness?

This esoteric question may become circular, just like the predetermination conundrum. However, there resides in *this* circular conundrum a grain of truth in that our *ideas* concerning a possible space-time continuum (and everything else for that matter) are themselves simply notions *within* consciousness. While some things or all things might potentially exist without consciousness (or outside of consciousness), our awareness of all things certainly exists solely *within* consciousness. This is beyond a doubt.

The riddle of the Eastern sages could be expanded to query: If all of the universe existed, but there was no Life and no Consciousness, would it really matter?

More emphatically, the gray-bearded Eastern sage might state in rhyming fashion:

"Whether the universe is filled with nothing,

or rocky debris.

It does not matter if no one can see."

The point of view of Consciousness is obvious, and it is inherently meritorious.

So, Consciousness, *can* be seen as one of the three pillars of reality, alongside space and time, yielding this triad:

- Space – containing matter (and thus all things made of matter).
- Time – containing (or rather enabling) events and interactions among material things.
- Consciousness – possessing awareness of these things and events, and capable of taking action upon them (and upon itself).

One might go a step further and say that consciousness not only possesses awareness *about* things and events, but by exerting some effect, consciousness also perhaps bears at least some degree of *responsibility* for the course of all things and events. If any of the three can be said to bear some responsibility for what occurs within the others, it is consciousness.

One could go so far as to theorize that a form of godlike consciousness willed everything into a gradually evolving existence. This theory takes the question to another level wherein we might have asked, "Which parts of the continuum are more responsible for the others?" Or, "Which of these pillars of the continuum might have more likely predated or comprised the others?"

Whether this theory (of a triadic continuum) is true or not, does not change the fact that we have a vested interest in the future, and that same future is influenced by our actions in the present. The culmination of our actions upon matter, events, and especially upon ourselves, can yet yield a form of super-consciousness (in the far distant future) that is indeed somewhat godlike in the degree to which it/we will be able to exert control over conditions (matter) and events (time). That embodiment of consciousness will indeed share the greater burden of responsibility for the conditions and events occurring within space and time. (It may be considered that this event would represent primordial or elemental consciousness more directly imposing itself into this physical reality via the widely dispersed conscious entities.)

The gravity of this heightened future state is perhaps that which propels all of time toward the future. It is this "ultimate state" that is perhaps the meaning and purpose of time. From the perspective of consciousness, it is the reason for the existence of all that is. It is the culmination of all our additive triumphs over all the struggles that have occurred and that await us still. In this ultimate state, there resides the resolution of all things, sitting alongside the amplification and magnification of all that is exceedingly good beyond all words.

This massive energy of Zenithity
Draws the conscious-laden universe
Curiously yet unyieldingly
In the direction of the future.

Counting Dimensions?

Just as we previously agreed to not get *too* bogged down over words and wording, let's not get *too* confused over classification and numbering schemes.

Accordingly, this next bit may be neither here nor there. But let's humor another thoughtful diversion.

Anyway, it may be useful, as a mental exercise, to review and break things down to fundamentals. It may be wise, to disassemble and reassemble everything we *think* we know – like a soldier disassembling and cleaning his gun in the field.

So, let's talk about these so called "dimensions" . . .

Sometimes, time is currently referred to as the fourth dimension. This is because space, before time was considered a "dimension", had been considered to be three-dimensional. Space was (and is) described as three-dimensional, because in our clever, boxlike, math-like ways of thinking, a unit of space could be 'measured' using three dimensions or directions *within* space.

Without a doubt, a three-dimensional coordinate system is useful for measuring an object, or the location of an object, within a region of space. Theoretically, one can address any point in space using a position on a scale along each of the three "dimensions": "Oh, Bob's house, which sits just up the hill there, is 84 feet in the x direction, 195 feet in the y direction, and 73 feet in the z direction."

Sure enough, using my front door as the zero point for the x, y, and z axes, we can mathematically deduce the location of Bob's front door using this coordinate system. But who is going to consider or effectively use an *infinite* three-dimensional coordinate system? It is plainly a mental construct that helps us understand our mostly localized space and spatial parameters. And while this system is useful for many purposes—such a choosing a box of the right size for shipping a lamp to Aunt Betty—it does *not* yield this conclusion: Since space can be theoretically measured using three linear coordinates, space is *therefore* comprised of three *very different* dimensions. That is an illogical conclusion. These are not three very different dimensions, they are 3 *directions* of measurement within the same dimension (space).

Basically, pretending that space encompasses three dimensions is rather daft considering that the three dimensions of space are really just three different directions at convenient right angles **within** space.

Sure, space is three-dimensional if you are simply defining a 'dimension' as a linear coordinate direction *within* space. But if we are calling "Time" a single "dimension," then we can't call space "three dimensions." Space is space—it is a unique domain that is limitless and unbounded in *every* direction.

Space, as a single vast dimension or domain, can be visualized in this way: Imagine the largest "piece" or section of space that you possibly can. Then take that and shrink it down to the size of a thimble. Surround it by yet *another* sea of even more infinite space. Repeat this over and over and you have space. All of that infinite space *is* (or should be considered) the *single* "dimension" of space as a corollary to the *single* dimension of infinite time.

Try to measure that with "coordinates."

Bottom line: Space, in all its infinity in every direction, even if this infinity can be measured infinitely in 3 directions, still counts as but one dimension (or domain). At least that is my position. Perhaps what bothers me, is the term 'dimension' that has been seemingly morphed to imply three directions in the element of space while describing as one the entire element of time.

Time, at least within this narrative, is also a single dimension—a single meta-parameter of pan-reality (just as space is but a single meta-parameter of pan-reality). Time is a dimension that is likewise infinite (linearly backward, perhaps funnel-shaped forward). Time is filled with the events occurring among and within all objects and beings.

Again, within this narrative, space is one dimension. It is one single meta-parameter. Space is infinite (in every physical direction) and filled with matter. Time is infinite, generally speaking, in two temporal directions, and filled with events.

So we have space and time; those are two dimensions according to how I recall as the normal way of counting. And if we must be hung up on considering space 3 dimensional, and time 1 dimensional, then perhaps we are again hung up over nuances of wording. So perhaps I should use a new phrase like "domains" instead of "dimensions" – so that I can make the logical point that space is one large domain, and time is another. And in so doing, others can continue describing space as three dimensions and relegating time as being only one.

But, for the remainder of this discussion, we will continue to use the term "dimension" as referring to an entire meta-parameter regardless of how that meta-parameter is divided or measured internally. And thus I will describe space as one dimension and time as one dimension. In any case, it may help to re-evaluate how we perceive these entities or containers.

Now whether to consider space first, or time first, is yet another quandary. This becomes a complicated or unanswerable question because time, in order to enable events among things within space, must first *have* things within space. According to that reasoning, space should or must logically come first. But how can any event occur across items in space (such as the *birthing* of all things within space) if time were not there first? A first event must occur prior to things existing. From that perspective, time should come first.

So, let's put a placeholder on that quandary, since from one point of view, time would be required to come first, and from another perspective, space would have to exist before time. If we must, as a tiebreaker, it seems that time would have come first – although I doubt we may ever really know with certainty.

So, in an attempt to be verbally and logically as descriptively accurate as possible, we might then say that we have a *time*-space continuum, instead of a space-*time* continuum. And, for clarity, we might assert that this continuum would consist of exactly two meta-parameters (time and space). We would in no way conclude that our continuum consisted of a single parameter of time and a "three-dimensional" parameter of space—which would result in time-space being counted as a total of four dimensions. That would be a laughable misuse of words and numbers, yet this is *ironically* how we now refer to these entities. Oddly, enough, without hesitation or question, we often now call time the "4th dimension".

Perhaps up until now, this chapter has all been an exercise in semantics. But underlying and key to this narrative, we are discussing a continuum into which we would like to propose adding an additional key element. We are aiming to include *consciousness* as an additional domain, meta-parameter, or dimension. Consciousness is an equal or greater dimension than either space or time, and it defines a domain that is clearly distinct from the other two. It is as amorphously infinite in sheer potential and range, and if we are to mull over its limitations, we must remind ourselves that it is only through the lens of consciousness that we can apprehend the other two (or anything really for that matter). And while some see it as a *product* of space-time (and of matter as well as of events), it can, from a contrarian viewpoint, seem slightly *more* likely that consciousness somehow yielded space and time and not the vice versa.

Certainly, the conundrum of, "you can't get something from nothing," is solved by this conceptual yielding of time-space from consciousness, or at least partially. For consciousness is not a "thing." At least, it is not a "thing" in the traditional sense. Consciousness is not a 'thing' of the same type as a thing composed of matter (toward which the "something from nothing" rule is normally directed). In other words, we might say that if Consciousness is a "thing," it is a "thing" of a very different type, and hailing from a different dimension or domain (other than matter which is an object within the domain or dimension of space).

For how can any events occur without time, and how can any things exist without space? Events and all interactions among things within space can exist only via time. So, it would seem that space and time were both borne of some "event." Yet how can there be events, without time?

At the very least, we can say that there was most likely an "event" of a type that we cannot conceive, which was outside the traditional events of time. That "event" (for lack of a better term) was possibly the manifestation of space and time by an act of a primordial type of consciousness: an unbounded, timeless conscious volition that spawned simultaneously both space and time. This is, at least, one possibility.

That 'unlikely' likelihood is no more unlikely than the development of consciousness via random events across a space-time continuum that *somehow* spontaneously self-generated. So, we can say that the likelihood of consciousness having predated space-time, or at least of coming into existence simultaneously with space-time, is just as strong as the likelihood of consciousness arising and developing into a form that may now ponder the imponderable beginnings of everything—having itself arisen randomly from a void wherein neither space nor time originally existed.

Every alternative seems improbable, or perhaps impossible. For that reason, it seems more likely that everything is of a conscious origin. The understanding of consciousness is the neglected "science" and therefore we know the least about it.

The reality of "*all that is*," so defiantly smacks into the face of impossibility that it can be considered a miracle from any perspective considered.

Everything, and even the mere awareness of anything,
completely defies the absolute of nothingness
in a manner that is miraculous by any measure.

This miracle, and everything that we know, likely came to exist via—and as—a vast series of rudimentary conscious constructs.

To make a long story short, Consciousness exists (without a doubt) and is a vital force within the universe (as has been and can be illustrated). So strong is the role of Con-

sciousness that we may begin to call it the 3rd dimension –
after space (the first and not three dimensions) and Time
(the second, and not the fourth dimension).

If we insist upon referring to space as three-dimensional,
then Consciousness can be considered the fifth dimension.
Fine with me. But it seems preferable to look at these meta
dimensions as individual "entities." Accordingly, we have
Time-Space-Consciousness.

If we believe that consciousness is superior, or super-rel-
evant, (or that it predates the other two) we might change
the order to:

Consciousness-Space-Time

or

Consciousness-Time-Space

But can we really count dimensions? Can we really measure them?
If we refer to space as three-dimensional because of x, y, and
z, but then refer to time as one-dimensional, doesn't that
cheat time?

Time exists as past, present, and future. Those "regions"
within the timeline are very *distinct*. They are not merely different points on a dumb line. The past has clear and distinct properties (as discussed to some considerable extent
previously). The present has a nature that includes properties uniquely distinct from either the past or future (for example, the entirety of existence resides within the present).

And the future is altogether a distinctly different and more probabilistic territory.

In short, time could be seen as having three distinct 'dimensions' that have distinctly different properties. These three distinct 'regions' of time are more akin to three different domains or dimensions than the three cardinal "directions" attributed to space and misappropriately referred to as "dimensions." If time were thus considered to have three dimensions and we retain the three dimensions traditionally associated with space, then consciousness would be considered the 7th dimension.

Lucky number 7 - sounds good.

But it is all just numbers that we are trying to use to fit everything into our engineering-oriented mindset.

To draw closure, the closest or best summary regarding what truly constitutes the continuum in which our reality exists is;

Three dimensions, consisting of Consciousness, Time and Space.

Does it really matter?

Perhaps it doesn't, but perhaps the exercise has put Consciousness on our radar in a way that it was not before.

And even if we don't consider it a co-equal partner with space-time and everything else, it is that domain to which *we* belong – like it or not.

OK, so, *outside* of this exercise, and outside of theoretical reasoning,
does it really matter?

> *What matters is that consciousness is real,*
> *and what's real is that Consciousness matters,*
> *and incredibly so.*

At Home in the Present

Back to timelines and such, let's begin to tip things ever so slightly in a different direction.

So, we have the infinity of space moving along a rail of time. But emerging from the present there are an infinity of forks in the railway leading into the future.

Without any steerage, the infinity of space would hurtle aimlessly down any one of the random future railways—propelled solely by the momentum of the past.

But let's recollect and refocus:

Does something else reside and operate within the present?

Bingo!

Consciousness, it seems, is quite at home in the present.

One could see it alternately,
that consciousness is pulling time through itself,
discarding the past and navigating the future so as to enhance itself.

Odd, but another question arises. What fills the 'realm' or dimension of consciousness?

Space is filled with matter, and all manner of "things." Everything that is anything, anywhere, exists somewhere within space. If we traveled across an infinite span of emptiness . . . on and on . . . we could then stumble upon another region, even more vast, and one populated by things and beings of impossible forms and descriptions. But the point is that space is filled (albeit sparsely in the quadrants known to us) with matter, things, and physical beings.

Time is filled with events, and all manner of change and interaction among things. Without time, everything would be frozen, stopped still. Even the molecules within all physical objects require motion, and changing our very thoughts requires time, so we can't really even imagine anything without time. Literally.

So space is filled with "things" (objects and matter).

Time is filled with events, change, and motion.

So, what fills the realm of consciousness?

Presumably, and for lack of sufficient wording, *consciousness* fills the realm of consciousness. We have no names for that empty place that is the abode of Consciousness as compared to the entity or entities of consciousness filling that place. Our understanding of consciousness is in *that much* of a state of infancy. We lack words to describe even the simplest of its attributes or relationships.

Perhaps this is a moot point; Is there a realm of consciousness wherein consciousness "resides"?

Perhaps, unlike time and space, consciousness (the realm) and consciousness (the entities filling that realm) *are indeed* one and the same. Perhaps we could use a different existing term for each concept. For example, "awareness" could be that which fills "consciousness," or vice versa. But for now, lacking a greater awareness of our own awareness, the words shall remain interchangeable.

And it is not beyond the scope of possibility that consciousness only exists within the physical world of matter (although I would suspect this is not accurate). But even if it does, consciousness, intelligence, feelings, awareness, and ultimately the "self" all constitute a fundamentally different type of "substance," and an essence or type of existence that is distinct from the material substances from which they are apparently derived.

To circle back to the main point, consciousness is real, and it matters. Perhaps more than matter, it matters. At least from our perspective, this will remain invariably so.

And to the lesser question—Where does consciousness reside? —we could approach it differently and say, "Consciousness abides in the present." As does matter. Matter in space, and consciousness (within the "conscious space"), both seem to reside in the present, yet are mutable or changeable over time.

> *But while matter is inert and pliable,*
> *Consciousness is active and aware.*

Perhaps this has all been stated and restated enough, and in so many different ways. I apologize for this if it has become tiresome or redundant, but I am attempting through this book to illustrate various esoteric ideas in a number of creative ways. As such, it may be more like painting a series of pictures, than it is like writing a literal and formal description.

In another light, we can try to enjoy this as a healthy mental exercise.

Also, as stated before, as a conscious being, you are able to reflect upon all of this further and come to your own conclusions, or you may make further extrapolations upon these conclusions and their illustrative summaries. That too is a wonderful thing.

It is also yet another affirming sidenote concerning the overarching importance of Consciousness and the *active*, rather than *passive*, nature it exhibits.

Without consciousness, the other meta-dimensions are meaningless, like the sound of one hand clapping.

These are merely conceptual models within the mind concerning the nature of everything. As such, these conceptual models can be further refined within the mind of the conscious individual, or within the public discourse (and ultimately within the broader context of consciousness as a whole). For on some level, the nature of our consciousness is evolving still. In the process of refining our understanding we may also further refine consciousness itself and effectively upgrade or enhance the properties it will then use to navigate conditions forever within the present.

As we navigate toward an ultimate future, Consciousness uses these and other types of speculative models to exercise itself and select the better futures, progressively.

Ideally, and hopefully, this will be so.

Regardless, in summary:

Consciousness exerts influence, across time, upon matter (space). Consciousness, over time, progressively alters itself, and becomes more adept at further wielding influence over space and matter both directly and indirectly.

The End toward which
All Things Are Drawn

If the future allows not only a linear path, but rather a "fanned out" series of probable pathways, then there are an enormous number of possible pathways moving forward from any juncture (each such juncture typically and successively known as "the present"). While the momentum of the current moment, as propelled by the bearing of all past linear moments, can conceivably cause a considerable narrowing of this fan, there remains an apparent infinity of alternate future pathways. The farther from the current moment, the wider the pathways diverge and thus a larger "infinity" of alternates exists—branching out, in one manner of understanding, from each subsequent moment.

Let's take the fanlike analogy of future possibilities further:

Conceivably, a greater number of divergent pathways will emerge and exist *sooner* as (or if) the restrictive pressures due to momentum from the past are lessened. (This lessening might occur conceptually or in reality.) And from another perspective, it is conceivable that the range of accessible future possibilities is *increased* or *hastened* by the power of consciousness across whichever means its will may be exerted. So it may be said that the accessibility of possible futures may have a direct relationship with the increasing power of consciousness (and its bearing by any means), and an inverse relationship relative to the power of the influence due to the momentum of the recent past.

I apologize, for it is uncertain if I am stating this relationship correctly, or if my wording is clear and accurate. Regardless, the relationship between consciousness and the future as well as the topic of the bearing of consciousness versus the influence of past momentum are of some value and worthy of further consideration.

In any case, we may reasonably envision the pathways of possible futures as being fanlike, but furthermore as having a potentially narrower or wider sweep or range of options.

Image #4—Possible Futures, Small Fan, Large Fan

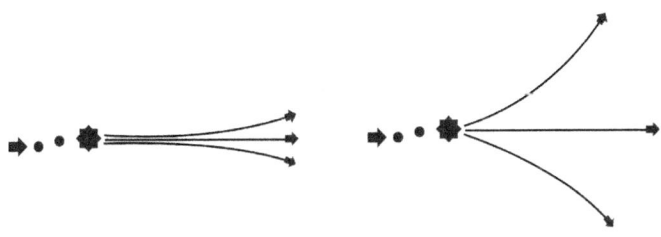

The fanlike nature of the possibility pathways may even bear an outward curvature, which in extremes could conceivably be imagined as "backward curving" or "circling back" to achieve conditions *similar* to previous positions in history. While it might be tempting to conclude that this is effectively a form of backwards time travel, rest assured that it is not. It is simply a theoretical crossing of the *new* timeline with a position that is relatively similar (almost identical) to a set of conditions along an older portion of the timeline.

Not only is this *not* time travel, but it is, more importantly, highly unlikely. It seems to represent the possibility of a retrograde or circular revisiting of *conditions* prevalent within a prior era. Such large-scale regressions would seem unnecessary, and they would probably be quite undesirable from the context of Consciousness (potentially delaying Zenithity). The notion is represented nonetheless, as a sheer conjecture in possibility.

Image #5—Unlikely Fan of (Immediate) Future Probability, Too Wide, Too Drastic

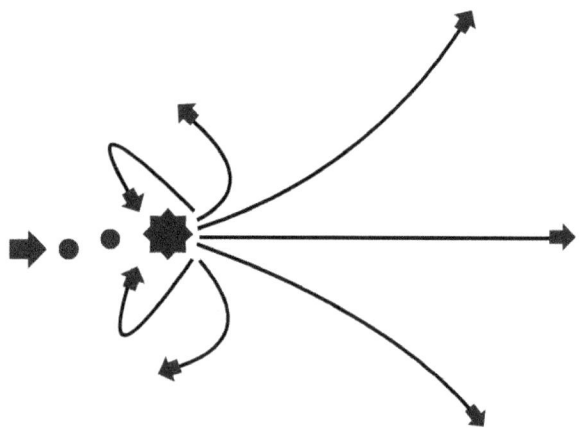

Certainly, no one knows the "width" of the actual probability fan at this moment, and from any future moment, a new (but likely very similar) possibility fan pattern exists.

Again, no one knows how wide the fan is at any moment, nor how to measure it. We are essentially comparing a conceptually larger set of infinite pathways (a wider fan) with a conceptually smaller-shaped possibility fan (with fewer infinite pathways). Some might say, "How can you compare two infinite sets of conclusions (or pathways in this example)?" Indeed, that becomes yet another unanswered and potentially unanswerable question. This type of equation, comparing two infinite sets, is said to be *mathematically* impossible.

Despite its defiance of our *notions* of mathematics (a greater infinity vs. a smaller infinity), a valid comparison of this type does conceptually and reasonably exist. The number of pathways that exist, although infinite, can apparently be larger in some theoretical instances than in others.

The net effects of this can be significant. Imagine a fan pattern that is relatively tight, almost like a pin, and barely tapered. *Eventually*, that gradual taper will yield an infinite width, whereas a broader fan pattern will achieve the same, infinitely large width much sooner, almost immediately in some circumstances.

Look at the comparisons of two infinite sets—one larger and one smaller. We can say that if we point two lines out in two directions, originating from a single point, then at some distance from the original point an infinite number (uncountable) of positions exist. This occurs even for two lines departing at an angle of just one degree.

Now imagine a similar point, with two lines radiating out at 90 degrees. Obviously, the infinite number of positions included between these two, more broadly angled lines occur much sooner. The infinity contained in the wider (90 degree) arc is clearly much larger than the infinity within the smaller (1 degree) arc, even though both are said to be immeasurable.

On the converse, the 1-degree arc reaches a certain infinite size at a certain infinite distance, but it is forever *denied* the 359-degree arc of infinite size outside of itself, which is *clearly* much larger. In fact, anyone can plainly see that while we are measuring or comparing two infinities (which is impossible to do, theoretically) that one infinite arc (359 degrees) is a significantly larger infinity than the other (1 degree arc), **and that the two are mutually exclusive**.

Image #6—Greater and Lesser "Infinite" Arcs of Possibility

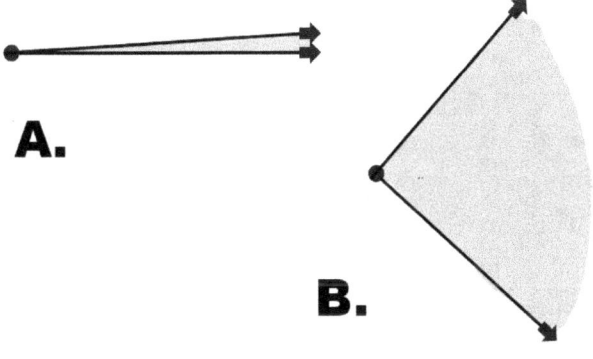

A. Relatively fewer 'infinite' possibilities included – much larger volume of 'infinite' possibilities excluded.

B. More 'infinite' possibilities included, fewer excluded.

So even in comparing volumes of a theoretically infinite nature, size *does* still matter. And logical comparative assumptions are still valid for a sentient logical being.

Just because something is impossible according to mathematicians, does not mean it is logically or realistically impossible. In reality, it exists; a greater and a lesser comparative infinity. So, in a funny way, I guess this is the closest I have ever come to doing the impossible – by merely stating that one infinity can be greater than another. I am sorry if that does not compute.

Clearly, the most important notion is that the wider the arc of possibility, the more options which exist. And those options which exist may occur sooner.

Generally, more options are a good thing. By widening the fan and increasing probability, the number of options available increases. But not *all* of the options are necessarily good. Let's say that with this wider range of options some are good, some are bad, and some are without much value in any evaluation.

But there will be a net total of more "good" options available in a wide fan pattern than in a tight one, and they will be available sooner rather than later. Much sooner, perhaps.

Again, if it is all random and without consequence, then by definition it does not matter. But it does matter. Why? Because *we* matter. Consciousness matters.

Consciousness will seek not only to widen the array of options (favoring a broad, fan pattern of possibility over a tight one) making many options available sooner. But then the utterly amazing property of Consciousness kicks-in: the ability to discriminate, to discern, and to choose. From among the wider array of possible outcomes, consciousness will progressively and selectively choose the *better* outcomes from the infinite array of possibilities. In essence, we navigate the probability field or fan in a proactive and positive manner.

In this light, Zenithity, due to its selectivity, can be seen perhaps as an inverse fan, acting against the possibility fan so that it becomes almost like a funnel—a funnel of consciousness, awareness, and logic. It becomes a funnel of reason, in effect narrowing or forcing the selection within the possibility "cloud."

Image #7—Theoretical Probable Futures as Refined by
Conscious Influence

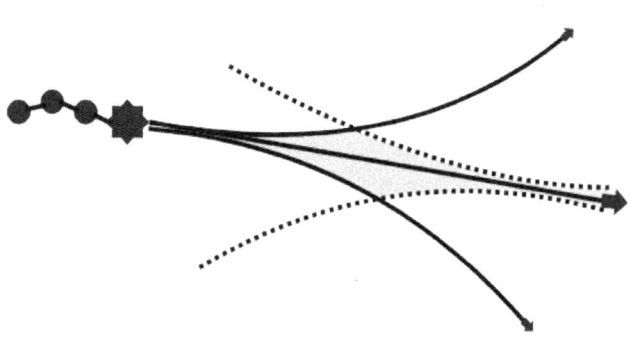

*(The dashed line represents conscious influence, with grayed
area representing resultant refined set of possibilities.)*

The pathways to Zenithity are like a funnel into the future, into which Consciousness focuses our very best inclinations, ideals, and outcomes.

This is the net effect of Consciousness over time:
an ideal possible future, toward which all things are drawn.

Consciousness, in this highly advanced state, may be said to be "godlike." In another context, it may be that God, in actuality, is thus more strongly manifest in the future, and as such we are drawn in the direction of time to Him.

The state of all things, at the hypothetical yet seemingly inevitable "conclusion," can be said to be a paradise that lasts unto the remainder of eternity.

Zenithity

Zenithity is a theoretical construct, a philosophical set of reasoned considerations and observations. As such, it is a hypothetical model that attempts to elucidate or convey certain key characteristics that apparently exist within the general nature of reality. It especially focuses on the probable favorable tendencies of future occurrences across this reality, and on our role in this transitioning state of reality as conscious beings.

At its core, Zenithity anticipates and represents
a perpetual zenith along the course of Conscious evolution
and the related development of universal physical reality.

Zenithity, while philosophical in some respects, can be seen from another perspective as a simple base-level belief system. It may be difficult to envision the theory of Zenithity as a full-fledged philosophy because the unmitigated, beyond-the-shadow-of-a-doubt "proving" of any *phi-*

losophy is nearly impossible and highly subject to personal interpretation. For this reason, all philosophies consist strongly in some measure of mere belief or perception.

However, if it constitutes a "belief system" moreso than a philosophy, unlike many other "belief systems," Zenithity does not stipulate a need for you to "believe" in it for its predictions and tenets to become actualized. It is not a belief system that works "only if you apply it." The theory behind Zenithity, at its essence, asserts (the possibility of) an inevitable progression of positive events which *will* occur due to the efforts and effects of Greater Consciousness, of which we are a part.

> *So if we consider Zenithity to be a "belief system",*
> *it is ironically a belief system*
> *that does not require our belief.*

While the premises behind Zenithity require neither your belief nor your intentional assistance, they necessarily rely upon *some* portions of a greater collective consciousness to make successful efforts to move in a progressively idealized direction. So, the self-directed efforts of individuals are not without significant impact. This is perhaps a finer distinction, but it implies that the net sum of the efforts of individuals (along with or as constituting any forms of Greater Consciousness) will lead to successively higher states of being and existence.

This assertation does not contain any language like, "This will occur *if* you believe in it." Or, "If you accept these premises, the following things will occur *because* of your acceptance and belief."

Zenithity occurs with or without you.

It occurs due to the *overall* orientation, disposition, and behavior of consciousness. Observable within Life, the existence of the powerful conscious element may be extrapolated across the cosmos—and perhaps additionally within alternate layers above or beneath our level of awareness.

But the formal process of Zenithity probably occurs so far into the future as to be reached without any of us who are alive today.

For now, a simple conceptual awareness will suffice to gently accelerate and enhance the initiation of the process.

This is because the process leading up to Zenithity *does* include you, at least in some small way. That is, it potentially includes any and every individual to some extent. Knowingly, or unknowingly, you are either contributing to, or detracting from, the eventual onset of this monumental process. Great job, right?

So, the process *does* imply that someone, somewhere, will be pulling in a generally positive direction. By the net effects of our actions, we are altering or modifying external and internal reality over time, in a direction that is more positive regarding Greater Consciousness. More importantly, Zenithity asserts that the net sum of all Consciousness will be pulling in a strongly positive direction (positive from the perspective of conscious Life). The results of this gradual amelioration will be cumulative, and will accelerate at some point, hastening a more rapid approach to an idealized set of circumstances.

But you, personally, (and please don't take *it personally*) do not have to believe in it, participate in it, or even be aware of it.

It will simply happen.

It will all occur quite naturally.

It is a "feature" of consciousness.

Can We Peek into the Future?

Some might ask, "Can we draw a clearer picture of what Zenithity will look like?"

At this moment in time, from our position with our feet humbly upon Planet Earth, the exact nature of Zenithity obviously can't be described in accurate detail. There is no concrete summary of *how* this ultimate state of cumulative enhancement will be. We do not know what it will "look like".

We are not making attempts at prophecy or divination, rather, we are attempting the art of logical reckoning, lucid use of imagination, and reasoned speculation. Yes, I know that some people hate the idea of speculation, but let's ease our fears of it for now since the *fear* of speculation seems to stifle creativity and imagination.

Moving on...

That idealized portion of eternity, which exists *after* the earlier portions of eternity, is entirely unfamiliar to us. That "paradisial" set of conditions, most likely existing in perpetuity in those future times, is beyond our capacity to understand now.

However, we *can* freely use our imagination, and let us not forget that imagination is one of the greatest faculties of consciousness.

But currently, we may only speculate about the nature of this state.

But is there any great harm in speculation?

For example, we could use our imaginations to consider, "What might be present in this idealized state?"

Perhaps within that exalted state resides the full realization of some very fundamental yet absolute ideals—such as love, peace, happiness, bliss . . . even excitement, fulfillment, and understanding. We can attempt to imagine a universe in which these principles are manifested, magnified, and fully exemplified or "fleshed out" within the existence of conscious beings.

These are among the first ideas which may jump into our minds as having overarching value and currently unfulfilled potential. Who knows what we might add to this very short list? Please do so with abandon, for imagining positive futures can be a healthy and relaxing experience. Also, one quickly realizes that the definition of an "ideal state" may differ from one person to another—and those differences too may become part of the equation. Certainly, an ideal state would encompass a variety of characteristics and broad-reaching activities that might pique the interest of even the most fickle and flighty. Or else some of us might suffer the agony of eternal boredom.

Or perhaps the qualities of our minds might change, such that boredom is no longer relevant.

But more likely, the types of things that we see as ideal, and the *ways* in which the ideals are manifested, will become more evident in the course of time. They will be manifested to the extent that our best expectations *today* are at best partial approximations of the eventual paramount circumstances.

The point is, to reach an idealized state, *all limitations*—even those that are merely hypothetical or which arise from a strictly contrarian point of view—would need to be overcome. This is entirely possible, and the theory of Zenithity asserts that this is not only likely but is fully *expected*.

However, only through the sifter of time will these notions be settled and understood.

That understanding, of 'exactly how any specific thing will be,' will not likely occur all at once. Instead, as we progress into the future, our understanding of each and every condition will gradually improve as we approach them individually. Cascading into the future, we will successively approach wave upon wave of "grasp horizons." As we approach some of these time-oriented grasp horizons (akin in some ways to *event horizons*), we will often gain increasing clarity concerning certain "future artifacts." Likewise, our notions regarding *how* we want a given "future artifact" to be, as a matter of refinement or elaboration, will sharpen. ("Future artifact," for lack of a better term, refers to any specific thing in the future; more specifically, it refers to a replica or construct of *how* that thing will *be* in the future—that is, the characteristics and interrelationships it will have.)

We might also envision the ultimate future state in terms of what it is *not*.

What conditions might be missing in an idealized state? What things might have been eliminated?

Sorrow, Illness, Death, Poverty, Hunger, Pain, Fear.

And, oh yes, the big one: Boredom.

Ok, Ok.

Perhaps boredom is not as heavy as the others. I mean, I guess no one has ever literally died of boredom.

And it *is* OK. It is OK to imagine what is best and what is worst and how the mitigation of those extremes might frame our progress via Futurology. At this point, our speculation is purely *subjective*, and it may be amiss. But in the course of time, the speculation and especially the honesty of our subjectiveness may *become* the point. That finer point being, that the subjective in some way transmutes and becomes the objective. This too is in part implied by the concept of Zenithity.

But for now, in our expectation of an idealized future, we might engage in a mental exercise to imagine a world without lack, or perhaps we might say, "Imagine a world lacking lack." We can attempt to imagine a Universe in which Consciousness has progressed and evolved a great deal, and the world of matter which could have become more subservient and productive to agile curation by futuristic forms of Life—perhaps our descendants.

Here too, we might also differ in opinion over what might best be lacking or missing in an idealized subset of the future. For example, perhaps there is a valid role for fear, lest we become too unguarded and thereby unable to fend off any very real issues that might arise. Who knows what unforeseen problems might arise to cause some very real 'trouble in paradise'? Hence, a measure of fear or caution might necessarily persist, even though our gut inclination would be that fear (or the need for fear) are unwelcome in our theoretical paradisical future.

But we must have a little *faith* that these and all other similar considerations will be taken into account, optimally handled, and in due time fully resolved. In the example of fear, perhaps our concerns will be absolved by means we can't currently imagine. For example, emotions like fear might cease while we reserve our capacity for dealing with the potential and the very practical sources of our fears. In our advanced state, this point might be moot, because we will likely have complete dominion over the objects of our fears—thus rendering them neutral.

But these are simply speculations about *possible* details within that inevitable super-conscious state which evolves during Zenithity. The details that we might envision are not inevitable. It is the idealized state that *is* inevitable (barring some inconceivable calamity of universal scope).

Try as we might, and try as we may, we really can't fully conceptualize what conditions might exist in this idealized utopian future. The point is, again, that *whatever* these idealized circumstances are, and *despite* our inability to perceive them, they *will* come into existence. They will occur via the gradual yet growing influence of Greater Consciousness across the universe.

Further conjecture on the matter, while a keen mental exercise and potentially enlightening, is not always directly productive nor is it necessary at this juncture. Suffice it to say, we are working or moving *toward* our ideals, and moving *away* from a state of chaos, confusion, fear, misery, and pain.

It is the origin of everything that is, was, and has been messy. It is through an eternity of progressive and categorical acts of organization of all the mess and formlessness that we have arrived here, at this *comparatively* advanced moment in time. This trend will continue, in an accelerated or expanded manner, into the future.

The future holds within it the potential for further refinement, exactitude, and "getting things right." The future represents the falling away of unneeded or harmful circumstances, and the undoing of broken or destructive prohibitions and inhibitions.

Life will reside in a much bolder and freer state in the future.

Awareness shines more brightly from its perch within reality so far ahead in the future.

Consciousness is much taller, fuller, better defined, and more self-assured as it beckons us into the future.

God himself (or perhaps more accurately "itself"), originally disparate and alone within the void, exists more distinctly and clearly in the future. That future, toward which we navigate and are invariably drawn, was in the moment of inception, His (and our) ultimate goal.

And these words, all of them, are but illustrations or markers pointing us to the notions or ideas that they represent. The understanding of these ideas (even though we are only partially capable of understandings of this magnitude) requires the *exercise* of thought, awareness, and creativity. And therein, perhaps, these illustrations can help us to imagine or perceive more accurately these possibilities and so much more. In some small way, perhaps these exercises help define the nature of our expectations toward a host of 'future artifacts' and other underlying conditions in the near and far futures.

The mind, like any muscle, must be exercised. The power of thought is benefited by its exercise. Of course, neither thought nor the mind is an actual 'muscle.' But from another perspective, the analogy is valid. We strengthen our thoughts through their exercise, and by pushing their boundaries. The validity of our thoughts is increased in concert with an increased capacity for thinking.

Empowered with thought, we can unlock many mysteries and discover hidden treasures. We may glimpse into the world of possibility, the world of probable futures both distant and immediate. We have, in thought, a most powerful tool at our disposal.

As we reflect upon these many things and more, bear in mind that it is the existence of our awareness that is the *greatest* miracle—the greatest aspect of Reality. The miracle is *your* individual, conscious awareness; that is a *greater* miracle than all of the dead matter, stars, rocks, and debris filling the entire universe.

> *As an entity possessing consciousness,*
> *awareness, thought and sentiment;*
> *You are the miracle.*

So, please consider again this concept of Zenithity, and if you don't like the name, then by all means call it something else. But consider the notion and what it represents, and consider all that it can be, and all that it could be. Consider, perhaps, that in fact it *will* be.

Consider it pro, and consider it con, but do not fail to include in your musings and considerations this notion;

> *By the sole determination and influence of Consciousness*
> *an Ultimate future is possible,*
> *perhaps even very likely,*
> *and some might conclude—almost inevitable.*

The Mechanysis of Perfunction

It may be difficult for us to imagine being part of a greater process, moreover a process of which we are not even aware. But we are (or we soon will be).

The Mechanysis of Perfunction is simply the sum of all positive actions by humans (and other beings of higher consciousness that might exist throughout the universe). While not all actions of conscious beings are positive, the net *sum* of these actions, over time, are (or will be).

It is an innate tendency of conscious beings to be drawn toward a greater good—if not the good of society as a whole, at least selfishly so, good for themselves. Even selfish advancement is, at least in some measure (and especially in survival or somewhat primitive situations), part of this vital process.

For a species to survive, its individual members must survive, or at least some of them. So a degree of selfishness is not necessarily a bad thing. One might even contend that some of our selfish interests or goals constitute a kind of rudimentary guide that's instilled within us—indicating our passions and thus driving our motivation. To the extent these can be mitigated against harm toward others, even our seemingly selfish goals and attractions can become a driving force for mutual reward.

As mankind and his situation progresses, more individuals will begin to make at least *some* of their decisions from a more selfless perspective. Individuals will begin to want what is best not only for themselves but also for their families, their social groups, their society at large, and ultimately the world to which they belong. It is easy to imagine that higher versions of selflessness exist beyond those listed, but we are probably not there yet.

But even today, depending upon the circumstances, it may appear that we have barely a shred of selflessness. Many of our outwardly "selfless acts" are seemingly committed for selfish reasons, often driven by the motivation, "What do I get out of it?"

That too can be part of this process. But eventually, as conditions (and our species) become more elevated, this gives way to a larger and more communal form of thinking. In time, the majority of our decisions and actions will become those that benefit everyone, collectively; for as the group advances so does the individual. Yet still, a fundamental sense of self (and an appropriate and necessary level of self-centeredness) will likely remain for quite some time.

So, despite the conditions or situations facing mankind, there will always be a tendency to advance above or through those conditions. This striving capacity of conscious beings is what drives (or constitutes) the Mechanysis of Perfunction.

The driving force behind Zenithity and the Mechanysis of Perfunction are the same, but the primary difference is that during the Mechanysis of Perfunction the positive forces are more diffuse and uncertain. There is a tendency during this epoch for humanity to take three steps forward followed by two steps back. But this is a process of ascertaining that our progress and direction are true and clear. This informalized process of attaining and ascertaining is characteristic of the era dominated by the Mechanysis of Perfunction, which leads to the more reliable and rapidly forward-reaching process of Zenithity.

In the Interest of Nomenclature . . .

The phrase "Mechanysis of Perfunction" is meant to provide a descriptive and memorable name for this exploratory and preparatory process. "Mechanysis" implies a process with a nature that is almost mechanistic or semi-automatic. It is not something that anyone is 'trying' to do right now, or has really attempted much at any point in the past. Yet the process of advancement is occurring, and it is a result of the direct action of pluralistic, discrete elements of consciousness.

The word "Perfunction" describes a process that is performed by the individual in an almost nonchalant or indeliberate manner. This is, and has been, the nature of progress; that it was not conceived or envisioned by one great leader or enforced and executed by some grim taskmaster. Progress occurs almost automatically as it is driven by the net sum of our *perfunctory* actions as individuals.

To clarify any confusion regarding the words "perfunction" and "perfection"; admittedly, the word "perfunction" sounds a lot like the word "perfection," and indeed, the theory of Zenithity does anticipate an "almost perfect" state (or process) that occurs at the end of the period dominated by The Mechanysis of Perfunction (a state of increasing refinement and elaboration). But the period embodying an increasingly "perfected" state occurs *after* a (potentially) more arduous and uncertain process. This unsteady process occurs in a somewhat perfunctory manner, gradually tending toward a more idealized state. The process toward Zenithity, via The Mechanysis of Perfunction, might be quite protracted, but situations will *hopefully* begin to progress geometrically during this timeframe.

We and other highly evolved lifeforms will have an increasingly lucid role in each of these processes.

A Taste of Things to Come . . .

Without a doubt, the future for mankind is a journey into an ever-expanding realm of both thought and reality.

This realm, as we proceed through it, will yield progressively richer and more vibrant outcomes. Likewise, these enhanced outcomes can and often *will* be embraced or appreciated by various individuals at every stage.

As time elapses, we will find ourselves in an ever more rapidly evolving succession of new states of existence. As a general rule, each successive state will supersede the previous state in many vital and rewarding qualities. The state of existence—for mankind, nature, and the cosmos (The-All)—will "evolve" along a path that some might call "progress."

By way of comparison, a given state many years hence will be seen as flourishing when carefully compared to related conditions many years in the past. The lot in life for a given individual is certainly more subject to random fluctuations regarding events and circumstance than is that of society as a whole. But moving forward, as each state of The-All flourishes, it will absolutely be the case that each individual will have a greatly increased likelihood of flourishing in a manner that roughly emulates, and emanates from, the increasingly enhanced state of The-All.

Back from the Future . . .

It is a fundamental tendency of mankind, nature, and The-All to progress or evolve to what may be seen as a progressively "higher" state. This tendency is significant despite the perceptions (real or imagined) of any individuals who may not "feel" as though they are existing in a relatively 'elevated' state of existence. This perception is partly due to our lacking, as we so often do, a valid point of relativistic comparison.

It is unclear why we are frequently unaware of the progress that is occurring or has occurred throughout our world. Perhaps, our disbelief occurs when looking back at some of the horrors and setbacks of history, we depressingly reflect, "The human race can never amount to anything. See what they did way back in 19-forgotten?"

Or perhaps it is in the day-by-day routine that we become lost in our perfunctory aspects of existence. We can't really "feel" how much better civilization is today than it was three hundred years ago, but if we really draw comparisons, it truly is in many if not most ways. That is not to say that there are not significant issues facing us globally and perhaps individually, and these are not to be trivialized. But on the whole, conditions are more favorable for most of us in today's world than they would have been five hundred years ago.

We can't experience a previous position on the timeline while within our current position in the timeline. Due to that, we might become somewhat jaded. When we are absorbed in the day-to-day struggle for existence, we become oblivious to the astounding opportunities and immensely rewarding lifestyles available to us.

Or, perhaps as we age, we begin to see our own lives as diminished. We may superimpose our personal aches and pains upon our perceptions of the world, even as it flourishes. This is not to say that the world might not encounter serious issues; within the span of one's lifetime conditions could easily go retrograde. But generally speaking, across time, we can see and appreciate the advancement and the progress. Especially if we choose to do so and willingly take off the blinders, we can see it very clearly. And if we try, it is not so very hard to see the positive *future states* awaiting us successively. But to see reality as fundamentally good, and becoming increasingly better, we may need to step outside of ourselves and look beyond our personal issues and hangups.

Either way, it is what it is—and we may choose to see it however we wish.

This takes us to where we are today, in the vicinity of that foggy and dreamy portion of the timeline known as "The Awakening Dawn."

The Awakening Dawn

The Awakening Dawn is so named because it describes a period in history in which mankind becomes increasingly 'self-aware', as if 'waking up' from a long slumber. This notion is nothing new, and many great thinkers, inventors, scientists, statesmen, and religious leaders who were 'ahead of their times' have described and ascribed to this notion of a rising state of awareness among mankind. Looking back at history, one may see scattered individuals whose lights truly shined more brightly against the dim backdrops of their respective eras. These people of great stature and prowess typically espoused a view that mankind is upon the brink of a great enlightenment. But perhaps the larger part of any 'enlightenment' belonged primarily to these rare and stellar individuals.

Much of our advancement and progress has indeed been contributed by a very blessed few. But in this new era during which we progress from "infancy" into "early childhood" (as a species), it will no longer be only a select few who act as if Life *matters*. Increasingly large numbers of people are contributing to this growing awareness like new stars popping into existence against a black sky. Eventually, it will be the rule rather than the exception that people behave, work, act, and *live* as if Life matters—because it *does*.

While the phrase "The Awakening Dawn" in this context may seem like a new usage, the very notion of a rising sense of self-awareness spanning the more recent portions of the timeline of the human species is clearly nothing new. However, whenever it occurs (presumably now, or quite recently) The Awakening Dawn is the juncture in our timeline when this idea begins to be ever more manifest.

What is it that makes the present a more viable period for this "increased awakening" than any point in the past? Why now?

Well, to be fair, "now" in this particular context refers to a timespan starting roughly five hundred years ago, continuing on through today, and foreseeably extending into the immediate future for at least ten years—probably another hundred years or so.

But does that really answer the question?

Why now?

It could be that a unique series of events has led us to the level of understanding that is required.

One of these long-term events is the increasing levels of education and literacy among large and growing masses of people. Intellectual stimulation and awareness can go a long way toward stamping out ignorance and irrationality.

Another of those events is the gradual realization that many of the superstitious tales of old are being seen for what they are; fairy tales and nothing more. Still, in parting with the distraction of fable, we must ensure that we do not lose the valid morals and values that often came along with these storied tales.

In addition to a fast-paced "falling away" of entrenched and ill-founded mistruths, we are beginning to see the limitation of the nation state.

This has been a bloody and difficult lesson . . .

Our species went first through tribalism, in which one small tribe often competed and fought sporadically over resources with adjacent tribes. They also fought doggedly over almost anything and everything, including the very right to be called a "human being." It seems that most ancient people believed that their tribe alone was "human," and that all others with different tribal customs and languages were not merely enemies, but "nonhuman," demonic beings.

Tribalism gave way to feudalism, a state in which one or more "noblemen" had risen above the din (usually by being more brutal than the next guy) and gained power over a whole region of local tribes. By this time, technology had increased minimally and, along with our increased learning in all matters, our skill in making war had increased as well. During this period, when one feudal lord chose to make war against another from a nearby region, the clashes were much larger and bloodier—partly due to the use of more advanced versions of the "pointy stick" (and other deadly implements).

The bloody era of feudalism gave rise to the even bloodier era of imperialism. In this era, competing empires covered large swaths of land governed formerly by numerous feudal lords or kingships. The larger and more advanced empires easily conquered and enslaved those regions that were still in a tribal or feudal state. But when these huge empires clashed among themselves, it was with armies at times numbering in the hundreds of thousands. The First World War can be seen as the final great clash of kings and empires. It was replete with death and destruction of every type: the hail of machine gun fire, explosives, aerial bombardment, choking gas, and fire weapons. Squalor and death abounded. Millions suffered and died needlessly supporting their own "favorite" empire." The alternative—being conquered by the *other* empire—was worse. However, during this era, a resentment and resistance began to grow. Those resisting asked, "Why am I being sent off into the trenches to die in this vastly exaggerated imperialistic squabble?"

The main remaining empires of the world saw their end with the conclusion of World War I, which was often called "the war to end all wars." Anti-imperialistic forces largely came to power among the advanced nations of the world after that war and took the form of republican, democratic, or communist forms of government. While these forms of government could certainly be seen as improvements over the absolute totalitarian monarchies which primarily predated them, nations still remained largely competitive and mistrustful of one another—and perhaps with good reason.

Sadly, the peace following "the war to end all wars" was short lived. Nation-states, self-impressed and emboldened by their own industrial advancement and their perceived stature above other nation-states, began clashing in ways heretofore unimagined. Armed by vast advances in industry and technology, then rallied by the belief that "our nation and our people are *the best*," the world plunged into World War II. By then the old kingships and empires were largely forgotten, but nation-states, and nationalism had risen up to take the place of the empires. Now the very large and technologically advanced nation-states could settle their differences on the battlefield on a scale that was beyond comparison—even when compared against World War I just twenty years earlier. Again, millions suffered and died, and the technology of killing surpassed our wildest dreams—or nightmares.

And then, that war ended, and it ended with quite a roar.

It ended with an atomic bomb – a weapon the splits the very building block of matter—the matter upon which *everything* is based. The nuclear weapon literally splits the very building block of physical reality, and that is a frightening and sobering thought.

So, why? Why *now*, are we "awakening?"

Because we have to.

We have to, and we must end wars somehow or we will all die. Even if we don't all die, we can conclude from reviewing history that wars have done little except stymie, set back, or delay our otherwise steady advancement. It ruins the lives of millions—or billions. And the ruined lives and timelines are *in addition to* the massive death tolls—for the catastrophes extend well beyond the dead.

In fact, we could say that were it not for the wars and the political oppression of tyrants, history would have been a mostly clear and steady march of advancement and improvement for humanity. Sadly, this march of progress, and the related happiness of millions, has been interrupted and broken too many times by war and oppression.

In a sense, we have been our own biggest problem.

Now, we begin to see: that this *must* end.

Other Reasons Why We Are "Growing Up" Now

Another reason this can be considered as the era of awakening is that we are now beginning to see that our lives and futures are intricately tied together on this planet. It seems that we are starting to "get it," to understand that individual human lives are important, even precious. We can empathize with one another—even across the globe. Our identities are increasingly bound more to the human species than to a specific tribe, king, nation, religion, or ethnicity. We begin to see that we have more in common, and for rational people, the differences between us seem increasingly trivial.

We are starting to realize that we are all human, despite our minor differences. Two arms, two legs, two eyes, one head, same blood, same genes—with perhaps only a few variations like skin color or hair texture. Is that worth fighting about?

Optimally, we can *help* one another—or at the very least help others by helping ourselves—so long as we do no harm.

We have begun to see (perhaps not fully yet) that we do not need to fight or kill everyone else over our ideals, our ways of life, our genotype, or our nation-identities.

To be clear, it is still a nation's right and duty to defend itself against unfair bullying or aggression by another, and this "tit for tat" may continue for a while. One of the worst possible tragedies would be for the world to fall under enslavement by an oppressive totalitarian regime in which all forms of progress (and the lives of all people) are thwarted. People—and nations—must be on guard and wary of that possibility. If necessary, good people must "fight back" to resist, by all means, any overly restrictive or oppressive form of control that hinders and retards progress. Abusive totalitarianism must be vigorously resisted whether it arises from within a country or arrives as an invading force from outside. People must, and will, carefully weigh *all* of these matters and decide accordingly.

But the idea that we could literally destroy everyone on this planet has now become a reality. An ever-growing number of people understand this fact in all of its ramifications.

Other factors, too many to list, have contributed to the heralding of this as the era of humanity's awakening. One important factor is simply the culmination of all the learning, all the science, and all the technology. Simultaneously occurring, the advanced and more realistic worldviews replacing impractical superstitious ideologies may be another factor. Simply stated, our knowledge of things and ideas has grown considerably across the course of human history. That accumulated body of knowledge, now available to the masses rather than restricted to those rare "literate" individuals, places us at a unique position in all of history. Essentially, now we are in a position from which we *could* become more conscious as a worldwide "species." At some point, since we *can*, and since it is advantageous to do so, we *will*. Hopefully this can occur before too many more wars erupt.

Technology itself is another factor. In the last sixty years, we have seen views of our planet from space for the first time, and we now witness that powerful psychological image regularly—the powerful image of what our world 'looks like' from space. It is an utterly amazing planet, filled with Life, and filled with utterly amazing people. The only difference is, now (as opposed to all of history up until about sixty years ago), we can literally see it for what it is. It is said that an image speaks a thousand words, and likewise that "seeing is believing."

Our awareness of the images of the entire Earth is doubly amazing considering that fewer than five hundred years ago major portions of the world were uncharted or completely unknown. At that time, we really did not know the full extent of the world, nor did anyone see it as it truly is. This is true both literally and figuratively.

Technology has also allowed us to communicate more freely. A network of thousands of satellites makes communication worldwide an instantaneous event. We can also travel more quickly and easily to any point in the world, and aside from a few unsettling experiences, we can come to realize that indeed we are all so very human. Beautifully human are we, in our very best light. And the better of our influences tend to "rub off" and "stick" to one another as we interact and observe our respective cultures.

Furthermore, simply having imagery (often "live" imagery) in the form of video and photography shines the light of awareness around the world highlighting any calamity, any issue. We can see—on our TV screens, cellphones, and computers—the scourges of war in real time. In increasing numbers, people are simply turned off to needless wars. The idea of killing a group of people, simply because you disagree with them, is increasingly no longer seen as justified. Instead, the court of public opinion often judges killing over ideology to be grotesque and atrocious—and thus the appeal of these types of conflicts (if they ever had "appeal") will certainly wane.

We can also see whenever a natural disaster occurs what needs to be done to help the victims, and how best to prevent or minimize such disasters in the future. By being more aware of the issues facing any portion of the world, we can analyze those issues and put them in proper perspective. We can investigate failed systems and underlying problems and make corrections as needed over time.

Through the power of image and video, we can also see all of the *good* that is happening in the world. People can see the smiles on faces of people in faraway places. We can share a friendship with someone across the world. We can consider the various positive attributes of various cultures, and even contemplate visiting or moving to those areas if we favor their conditions over those of our own locale. Ultimately, we can merge the *better* attributes of all cultures, and leave behind as 'history and tradition' those aspects that are less than appealing (for example, human sacrifice and slavery).

We can also see the regions rife with poverty and other problems related to a lack of development. It is important to note that learning about conditions by "seeing" (in a photograph or video) is so much more powerful than hearing or reading about them. We are in an era wherein the eye of the camera helps keep the evil, and the "backwardness" in check. Just as darkness abhors the light of day, evil even more so abhors an ever-present witness in the form of ten billion cameras.

In short, it may be the sheer growth of our collective awareness, most of all, that is allowing us to "awaken." It is our realization of what is going on in the world on a much wider scale that makes us recognize that each of us has *some responsibility* regarding the making of the future via the present.

Let us make it right.

Comparative Logic and Reason

In our current day and age, we, as individuals, are usually unaware of the gradual progress occurring on a universal, global, or even a local scale. We are not usually even aware of progress occurring within the lives of people who live nearby, much less do we even begin to notice all the major and minor advances occurring in the lives of people around the world each and every day. Most of us are only keenly aware of our own struggles, and of the gradual successes we have in prevailing over our own personal issues.

While it would be "really cool" to be somehow "hyper-aware" of all the progress being made each day, in every corner of the world, we know this type of awareness is not really possible for us as individuals.

Luckily, it is not required or necessary: Progress does and will occur all the same.

Progress on the Larger Stage

Some of us, having slain most of our personal "demons," might wonder,

"How can *I* be part of the larger process of progress? How can *I* contribute something significant to the "bigger picture?"

The best way to ensure that our effect is for the greater good is to make sure that your own experience of life, and your contributions to Life within your own immediate sphere of influence, are generally more positive than negative.

Certainly, it would be awesome if each of us could be a truly great and influential person having a towering global influence. But it is neither necessary nor realistic that each person should have overarching influence or fame.

If we can find an inner happiness in this life, then we have made astounding progress, and we have contributed our worthy sum to the overall advancement of the condition of Life.

That is enough.

Good enough.

But that doesn't *directly* answer the initial question, does it?

Even though the enhancement of our own state is *the* most fundamental step in affecting greater circumstances in a positive way, some may wish to act more directly to affect the progress of the human condition. Still, it is best to get one's own personal house in order before moving on to bigger and broader challenges. Otherwise, the "greater good" we intend to provide may be somewhat tainted by our own unsettled and discolored misgivings.

The next simplest step is to begin locally, or within the lives of those closest to us. Trite and predictable as this may sound, it is where the most meaningful impacts are often made. The truly great achievements often begin with something simple or localized in scope.

Basically, if you can make the lives of those around you just a *little* better, perhaps in a manner similar to the way you have improved your own state, then those accomplishments may seem to occur almost naturally.

This will become your second great accomplishment.

If something has worked for you, if you are good at something that has brought you success in any area, then perhaps it will work well for someone else too. It can be helpful if you lend your assistance, bringing your skills, knowledge, or good influence to bear within an area of focus.

Perhaps those old personal "demons" you have conquered were just "target practice," priming you for the larger and more difficult task of helping others eliminate their similar fears and other forms of baggage.

Often, by simply having a joyous and positive nature, we automatically affect those nearby in a positive way. So, indirectly, by virtue of the first great accomplishment (a very personal accomplishment), we often inherently affect those around us. Essentially, the second great accomplishment can occur by default—without any additional actions or efforts needed.

Regardless of the form of your localized personal contribution, by successfully providing your help or expertise, even if to only a few, you will have made a meaningful impact that extends beyond yourself. In so doing, you have exceeded all normal expectations and raised the bar to new heights.

Finally, if one can perform a *truly* greater act of good which *clearly* benefits broader humanity, then that becomes an undeniably elevated or exalted accomplishment. Your successful efforts will have taken you far above and beyond the call of duty. This third great accomplishment naturally results in an improvement in *any* of the conditions of life. Whether or not you are rewarded in any material way, it is nonetheless to your eternal credit. For that great feat, may we thank you in advance.

Regardless of which "stage" upon which the advancement occurs, the primary rewards for all advancements are inherent and internal. The invaluable rewards for attaining higher goals are largely self-realized. Priceless.

Lacking any significant downside, there should be no hesitancy toward any of them—especially when the insight is available and the opportunity is present.

Dare to Compare

Advancing oneself, those around us, or the greater good of civilization—these are not always easy. While it is easy enough to enumerate goals or guidelines, it is not always apparent how to achieve the necessary results.

For one might rightly wonder *how* to accomplish even the simplest of these feats.

Some might wonder, "*What* is it that *I* can change?"

Or more importantly, "What, if anything, *should* I change?"

Stated more explicitly, "What would be best for me to change, and how, and why?"

While these questions seem simple and straightforward, they are broad-based and might have *many* potentially correct answers. Over many years of reflection, I believe I have observed, isolated, and distilled the most direct answer from among the various fundamental perspectives which have emerged. In sparing you the laborious process of elimination and the details of years of analysis, I will proceed with the simplest and most reliably practical answer.

Concerning *how* to progress, or knowing *what* to advance, here is the key:

The easiest way to move from a lesser state to a greater state is via *comparative reason* (or comparative logic). This is a natural capacity with which we humans (as rationalistic conscious beings) are natively endowed, so it can actually be quite simple.

Examine a condition in your own life. Then look out into the world to see how someone else is handling the same condition in a better way. Or look for someone who has changed that condition altogether for the better. Maybe assume that someone, somewhere, has solved this type of problem before. Certainly, there is someone who does not have the exact same problems as you. If not, then why not?

Also, if there are people who *have had* the same issues as you, but who no longer do, then what did they change? Comparatively speaking, how did they avoid or resolve the same issues which now confront you?

Here is what not to do: continue plodding through life, year after year, struggling with the same old, tired, and broken-down issues.

At some point when we "let go" of our prideful resistance and rise above the ego, we can look out into the vast flock of humanity and often find that scores of other people have already conquered problems quite similar to our own. A solution or recipe often already exists. By a simple act of comparison, and a little opening up, we find that we can more fully 'join the human race.' By accepting and embodying the best traits shared by our fellow man, we can freely employ the solutions and upgrades that others have already success-fully demonstrated.

The significant observation here is that we often fail to use our faculties of comparative logic in the circumstances where they might matter the most.

It's odd that we are diligent in using comparative logic when buying a television or when deciding which can of peas to buy. But somehow, we are unwilling to apply com-parative logic to the things that matter most within our lives—like our beliefs, habits, thinking patterns, and routine behaviors.

We often fail the most tragically and enduringly when we fail to apply the simple act of comparative logic to our more significant ongoing problems.

Is it not obvious that by consciously comparing one set of conditions to another we *can readily become aware of* which is better? At the very least we can achieve this comparison within the context of our own (very valid) personal estima-tion. Then, if it seems feasible and desirable to change to the alternate (better) set of conditions, then one may freely choose to do so.

Obviously, *effort* may be involved, but as long as the rewards exceed the effort (and assuming no unforeseen calamity ensnares the process) then the effort will be worth-while. In the long run, you will have improved the associated aspects of your own life.

The chief idea is that whatever the condition you wish to improve, a recipe probably already exists for improving it. Just look around, do a little research, and your mind, which naturally excels at comparative reasoning, will fill in the blanks.

This can apply to purely mental or attitudinal issues as well as to practical, physical issues. If you can research and discover a way in which other people have managed a personal issue differently from the way you are handling the same issue for yourself, then you have a ready-made comparison. For some types of common issues, self-help remedies and support groups, of all types, exist across all mediums.

Likewise, if you just want your roof to stop leaking,
It's a fairly sure bet
that you can find someone with a dry attic.
Via comparison, it should be an easy matter to figure out
how and why.

Alternately, if we choose *not* to compare or to use reason, then we will most likely be stuck in our own personal set of stagnant conditions. There entangled, we will essentially be passively waiting for random events or for some external occurrence to "magically" intervene and change our conditions for the better. This is a form of fantasy thinking in which we subjugate personal responsibility to, often imaginary, external forces. Regardless of the reasoning or lack thereof, unless our lives are perfect, we can usually benefit from simple acts of comparison.

So, comparative logic is really quite simple. One might even 'make the case' that it is the basis for the majority of progress that has been made by the human race to date.

It's about 90 percent "monkey see, monkey do."

Truthfully, using comparative logic and reasoning can be that straightforward—aside from making the effort and any actual work involved. And of course we know that some people are allergic to anything that looks like work. But that too is an ailment that can be cured. It has been done before by millions of people who have transformed themselves from lazy to light speed.

Dare to compare.

But again, while employing reason is simple enough, it is our failure to apply it to our more significant situations that perpetuates the greater of our distresses.

Comparative Hypothetical Reasoning

From the previous conclusions involving the comparison of one existing situation with another similar one, the following line of questioning might appropriately arise:

If all progress occurs from looking at another similar situation, determining if the similar situation is *better* than our own, then copying that situation—how does everything *really* get any better? Seems like at some point no one will have a better way of doing anything since everybody will already be doing everything the same way.

Well, this is where the *real fun* comes in.

Comparative logic does not rely only upon *real* situations for purposes of comparison. Comparative logic can be applied with equally powerful effects using *hypothetical* situations or conditions. The *imagination*, another innate quality of human consciousness, can quickly and easily provide creatively derived sets of comparable conditions.

The simple act of logical comparison is the same, but when using hypotheticals, you are not literally comparing your set of conditions with those of any other person. You are making a much greater leap of *creativity* (another latent capacity of Consciousness) and imagining an entirely *new* set of conditions.

Wow! It is all quite obvious, but still, when you think about it, it's truly quite amazing. We can *actually* do this; it is a superpower that we all have.

Here's how it goes, in case you do not know.

The comparison occurs within your mind, which envisions or conceptualizes a fair and clear portrayal of *how* the newly conceived solution *might* perform (in reality). This hypothetical set of improved conditions is compared—*solely within the mind*, mind you—against the current set of flawed conditions. The comparative logic occurs entirely within the analytical mind. Best of all, this occurs *before* we attempt to implement the actual improvements. So we can evaluate multiple sets of improvements, escalate each through a hypothetical implementation, and then—and only then (and only if desired)—enact the sole improvement that appears to be the best.

Amazing, right!?

We take this for granted, but it is a true superpower.

It is a very simple but latent superpower that might be underutilized by many people.

If luck is on your side, and if your imagination and reasoning capabilities are working properly, you can and *will* make a considerable leap forward—comparatively speaking.

You will have envisioned a set of conditions that can be better than your existing set of conditions.

Furthermore, these entirely new conditions, which you have deduced via your own volition using a native capacity of consciousness, may be better than the related set of conditions facing most other humans. In this scenario, you will most likely become the person who is being copied—the "copy-ee" rather than the copier.

Societies, cultures, and nations (via their individual members) can likewise use comparative logic on a larger scale. They can and have done so throughout history, for this is how much of our shared progress has occurred. But the *real* progress has almost always occurred at the hypothetical stage first; that is, someone had to actually **think** of something first, before everyone else could copy it. Of course, that "something," which was "dreamt up" by "someone" would need to be *worth* copying.

> *So, initially, it is not ever;*
> *"Monkey see, monkey do."*
> *That always comes later.*
> *Instead, it must always first be;*
> *"Monkey think, monkey do."*

Later, one culture might look at another and say (if cultures could speak), "Hey, we like what they are doing over there. We don't have that type of 'great fun' over here. We don't have the same type of progress or advancement that they do. Let's try doing some of what they are doing. It seems better. Not in every way, but at least in some ways. So, maybe it is worth a try."

While we are sometimes taught to be somewhat hesitant in comparing "cultures," there can be an advantage in doing so. This assumes, with the best of intentions, that we have something to learn from each other's cultures. If one culture has characteristics that are "better" or more desirable than another's, won't most people prefer to emulate the former? Naturally, it is decidedly so – and it happens all the time.

In fact, this concept of comparative hypothetical reasoning, when vigilantly applied, is perhaps what allowed some cultures to become more advanced much more rapidly than others. It allowed them to essentially be presented with the exact same scraps of information but to put it all together in a more *reasonable* and productive manner, unfettered or unhindered by preconceptions or societal pressures. It would seem that the formalization of rationalism, the age of reason, the enlightenment, and all related philosophical achievements indeed fostered all the unprecedented scientific, technological, and cultural advancements that followed.

In light of this, it seems that our reasoning may be most powerful when we are *able to be skeptical* enough to suspend or disallow what we are taught or conditioned to believe, yet *creative enough* to devise entirely new explanations when existing conditions are lacking. Finally, we must be *disciplined* enough to pursue the implementation of any improvements that we may have deemed to be promising.

On the other hand, when we fail to use our capacity for comparative hypothetical reasoning, *we will fail*, in that our problems will endure for a comparatively long time.

Vigil-Mind

When an individual frequently uses comparative logic or reasoning—so often that it becomes a natural part of daily life, we might call that "Vigil-Mind."

In the state of Vigil-Mind, an individual becomes acclimated to using comparative logic (using existing real or imaginary hypothetical alternatives) almost constantly. Individuals in this state are always looking for ways to improve themselves personally and to improve the conditions within which they find themselves. By association, they very directly improve conditions for their families and closest companions, and since they are often copied, they also provide indirect benefits to their peers and contemporaries who naturally emulate their more successful attributes or accomplishments.

Comparative logic and "Vigil-Mind" may have existed in an obscure or unrecognized form since the dawn of man, but at this time, it seems appropriate to give this way of thinking (actually it is more a way of "being") a name.

For the individual, for his family and those around him, for his culture, his nation, his world—Vigil-Mind entails a *responsible* state of mind that propels individuals to the limits of their capabilities.

The advantages that accrue from Vigil-Mind are abundant and become quite evident, while it remains a practice which is a virtue unto itself.

When one engages in reasoning very regularly, one becomes a slightly more conscious participant in The Mechanysis of Perfunction, even here during these humble times (The Awakening Dawn). By so doing, in some small measure, one may hasten the onset of Zenithity (an ultimately benevolent process and state), and in the meanwhile, may contribute to the betterment of one's own sphere of existence.

In simplest form, here is a summary of what must be understood in the here and now;

1) Reason, Comparative Logic, and Vigil-Mind all lead to advancement.

2) Advancement yields benefits.

That's the short list.

That *should be* all we need to know.

In a broader sense, Vigil-Mind encompasses more than just reason and logic.

Within this practice there is a fairly constant effort to question, apply reason, open oneself to options, test and requestion these ideas, and so on. It is a concerted effort to find answers, solutions, and the Truth.

In essence, Vigil-Mind is a state in which one simply *allows* reason the *opportunity* to prevail.

It is also a state in which reason and logic are well balanced by a sense of appreciation.

It is a state in which applying reason is tempered by a sense of awareness and mindfulness.

It is a state wherein there is a flourishing open-mindedness and a sense of curiosity about the world and everything in it.

It is ideally a state in which spontaneity and creativeness are heightened and not stifled by the perceived rigors of logic and reason.

It is ideally a state in which decisions are made, not only based upon one's own individual needs but also by taking account of the wants and needs of others, and The-All.

The Principle of
Proportionate Good

In light of how we can seemingly progress as individuals, and seeing how this seems to translate into a generalized progress in conditions for our species as a whole, it sometimes seems that a subconscious "guiding force" is subtly embedded within nature. Or maybe there is another type of "guiding force" floating free form within the cosmos. Or perhaps our capacity for progress, and our tendency toward it, are simply innate properties of Consciousness (of which we are an ever-advancing part).

Progress may be seen most simply as a person, or a collection of people, going from a state that was worse to one that is better. This is the purest way to view "progress."

Any person with the type of consciousness that we consider "human," can easily see that indeed various things in life are "better" and others are "worse." Whether these conditions may be the results of great international events, or matters of a deeply personal nature, it is "self-evident" that there are degrees or relative levels of that which can be described as "good" versus "bad."

Defining or laboriously distinguishing "good" from "bad" in an esoteric way is not the goal at this juncture. Similarly, relating to these types of value judgments as merely "relative" does not serve any purpose in this discussion, as we are not defining a moralistic conception of "good versus bad." We are attempting to apprehend, from a subjective point of view, the very real value judgments pertaining to various events or conditions.

The fact is, there are conditions or events which any conscious being would describe as "good" or "better" when comparing them with certain other events that could conceivably be seen as clearly "bad" or "worse." For example, having your hand hit by a hammer is absolutely and without uncertainty, worse than eating a pleasantly tasty morsel (presuming the morsel was not harmful in some foul way). Enjoying a nice walk in the park is clearly *better than*, let's say, having a brick dropped on your head.

Any logical person can easily, and will readily, make this type of comparison under all types of circumstances, without any degree of uncertainty or hesitation. Happens all the time.

These seemingly obvious points must be made, because the notion of relativism (while valid in some contexts) has crept into our formerly rationalistic outlook in a somewhat detrimental manner. It is important to note, as evidenced by the former examples;

Relativism does not really apply to the bulk of our experiences.

The premise, at this point, is that each person perceives events and conditions as varying in extent and ranging from good to bad. Clearly, within that realm—wherein a good or bad event (or condition) is *possible*—a range of gradated or incremental differences exists between two extremes, consisting of an infinity of *possible* better/worse comparisons which can be stacked in order. This "sliding scale," which compares conceptual events (or conditions and states) as "better or worse," results in a representative ladder of almost unlimited height and depth. The intervals or "rungs" on the ladder are represented by an endless number of real and potential conditions and events (many of them quite complex and universal in scope). The rungs of the ladder (consisting of all possible conditions) are plainly organized in order of "worse to better."

In practice, our ability to evaluate differing conditions may sometimes turn out to be incorrect. Or at other times the distinction between two choices is so minimal as to be imperceptible. Furthermore, the choices we must make in day-to-day life may sometimes yield dilemmas within which the better of two choices becomes somewhat complicated or vague.

Despite these "gray areas," when comparing two sets of conditions or choosing from two choices of actions, the premise of "proportionate good" is subjectively undeniable. All conditions (or events) have comparable levels or degrees of good versus bad (or positive versus negative, happy versus sad, and so on). This could only be denied by someone who is obstinate or bent on pedantic argumentation. And even those arguments would arise only from hollow academic posturing and not from the very real and relevant sentiment arising from genuine subjective consciousness.

This Principle of Proportionate Good will be understood more clearly one day. With that clarity will come the understanding that it is not only true in "perception" or in a merely relativistic manner. Obviously, we could say that "everything is relative" and in so doing we can negate any concept, or any principle ever conceived. In the meanwhile, for the individual, the results are apparent and can be witnessed within one's own personal experience.

Ironically, in some ways, the Principle of Proportionate Good indeed defines a *subjective* system wherein one condition is *relatively* better or worse than another.

So, please let us not try employing any tardy or limping argument of "relativism" against this principle, whose validity should be embraced as ever so obvious. The point is, in several fields of thought, the subjective is *all* we have. If we eliminate everything subjective, then we might as well eliminate the entire endeavor of attempting to understand consciousness or any of the related disciplines.

Just because something is subjective does not mean it is invalid, especially when that which we are discussing will be *inherently* subjective.

Having understood and accepted the Principle of Proportionate Good, we can draw some additional conclusions:

If some things (conditions, events) are *better* than others, and we can (theoretically) stack all conceptual things (conditions, events) in ascending order of "worse to better," then there will be a directionality in this scale toward which all conscious (subjective) entities will naturally tend. All conscious entities will tend toward that which is better than that which is worse.

Yes, there will be variations and exceptions. Of course, not all behavior will ascend according to this unseen 'scale.' Still the general tendency and the direction will be positive or ascentive.

Furthermore, if we closed-mindedly assume that there is a flatly limited "top" to this scale, we can envision the uppermost rung to which we may ascribe. But if we more realistically assume that this "worse to better" stacking of all conditions and events is *infinite* in either direction, we will instead ascribe to the following notion:

There is a good that is infinitely ascendant.

In our immediate lives, we need not be concerned with understanding or directly knowing the infinitely ascendant good. It lies so far above and away as to be beyond our capacity to envision. But it is comforting to know that, conceptually, there *is* a good that is infinitely ascendant. It is nice to know that there are layers upon layers of heretofore unimagined states and conditions that are far above and beyond those which we have yet dared to imagine. And those auspicious and esteemed states exist far before (or beneath) that state which is infinitely ascendant (the Ultimate), and considerably after (and above) our current state.

We need not ponder and wander for too long in our imagining of those distant places and times so far ahead. In the here and now, we need only be concerned with knowing, in our own spheres of influence, what is generally better than worse. And knowing or determining, of those better conditions or states, which ones are actionable or achievable.

Perhaps that's the beauty of it all. We do not need to navigate by considering distant unknowable conditions that lie far beyond the horizon. Instead we may simply navigate by discerning those *nearby* conditions or states and evaluating and choosing the better from among them.

I won't deny that *some* degree of relativism may apply. In certain situations, one's personal selfishness might be expressed in the determination of what is "better and worse." This is to say, what is good for one, *in some circumstances*, might indeed be bad for another.

While this tendency is more relevant in the more distant and primal direction, as we move in the direction of the higher applications of "greater good" and "greater truth," those selfish goals become replaced increasingly by universal truths and goals having collective or overarching value and benefit. We would expect this to occur naturally as we move upwardly along the scale.

And again, we are not necessarily discussing the *moral* implications of one person's "worse to better progression" as it may impact another's. The Principle of Proportionate Good is simply stating that within our very real yet subjective experiences, there exists an infinite series of "worse to better" sets of conditions, states, and events that are possible. By individually following these naturally reasonable comparative conclusions in a localized manner, we all tend to humbly progress toward that which is better. It can be imagined that our cumulative progress might hopefully "ratchet-up" considerably at some point in the future. Optimistically, that point might occur sooner rather than later.

As we approach the infinite apex (a nonreal apex) of the ladder of proportionate good, we may easily visualize a realm in which universal Truth and the universal good proportionately negate and overshadow *entirely* all the far lesser "rungs on the ladder." And since there is no true "apex," in the ladder's infinite nature, there are "rungs" that far exceed the nearly utopian set of conditions already described (even if described ever so briefly, scantily, and with futility in grasping for elucidation).

Thus, arising from the Principle of Proportionate Good, is the Theorem of Ultimate Good.

The Theorem of Ultimate Good states simply:

A. There exists an ultimate set of conditions that is comparatively better than all other sets of conditions.
B. Furthermore, this set of conditions is not necessarily subjective, nor is it derived from a given perspective, nor does it merely arise from a given perception; instead it is a distinct and absolute set of conditions in an idealized, yet very real, sense.
C. But since all sets of conditions are infinite, yet still stackable in order from "worse to better," there are yet additional states that exceed that highest estimable state. Subjectively, the state of Ultimate Good is that highest estimable state which we can realistically conceive.
D. Conscious entities will always individually and collectively *tend* toward, and *aspire* to, the Ultimate Good: that infinitely distant apex in the comparative ordering of conditions and events from "worse to better."

Within the concept of Zenithity is the central notion that Consciousness is innately or naturally drawn toward this "apex" of Ultimate Good, and *when* that process reaches a certain point the further progress becomes nearly irreversible or inevitable.

In another light, the mere presence of consciousness, especially Greater Consciousness, makes the future-forward portion of the process inevitable at *any stage* within the process.

The Miracle of the Moment

There is a particular portion of the timeline where we spend *all* our time. It is often called the present, but "the present" often refers to a whole period of time (like "the present era"). Therefore, in order to clarify, there is a *part* of what we might casually call the present wherein consciousness exclusively resides. This immediate part of the present is what we casually refer to as "the present moment," or simply "the moment." Everything occurs within *this* specific and *active moment*. It is in *this* precise yet very fluid and *active moment* in which we and everything else perpetually exist.

Literally, we are *always* within the present moment, and it is in this moment (the now) that all action takes place. We cannot define how long a single moment is. While it resides upon the timeline as but a pinpoint—always moving, its contents always changing—it is still just a pinpoint on the timeline. Again, bear in mind, that this "pinpoint" contains the net sum of the universe and all known forms of consciousness. But the moment, at best, is but a momentary, "moving" snapshot of those constituents. In a greater sense, the moment is the living, breathing, active vehicle of The-All. It is like a forward-moving bubble encompassing everything that is real.

How long is the present moment? As soon as we have paused to observe it, it is gone—replaced by another. The past always steals the moment, or so it seems.

An individual moment occupies no real distance upon the timeline, yet through this lone pinpoint or "bottleneck" *all* change occurs. While all change occurs within the moment that is present, the present moment continually progresses through time. So, from another perspective, the immediate moment, in which we reside, stretches on and on throughout eternity, constantly transforming the past into the future.

So, from one perspective the present is infinitely small in the direction of time, as it interfaces between the rigid past and the flexible future. And from another perspective, by (eventually) spanning and essentially creating every "moment" that ever was or will be, the immediate moment is in some ways infinite *across* the span of time. The present moment never ends, since it is *always* here. It is always now.

As such, the moment may be seen as fundamentally "miraculous," for quite precious indeed is this moment and every moment in which we perpetually reside.

We could call it; the miraculous moment.

When we fail to realize the miracle of the moment, we deceive ourselves into denying our most fulfilling future.

When we fail to appreciate the moment, in some way we have cheapened that moment, never to regain its opportunity or splendor. Always in our own history, that particular moment will remain etched as forever blighted or amiss.

But we always have at our disposal, or rather at our opportunity, a new moment. A new moment arises—now and always. In *that* moment, we can get it right. This is the ever forgiving, ever flexible nature of our time-based reality. We don't need to go back in time, as some would seem to wish, in order to "fix things" (or more likely to inadvertently "ruin things"), because we have been given (via the construct of the medium of time) the *perpetual* opportunity to "fix things" in the moment, in the present, in the now.

We can always try to honor each new moment, and in so doing we can add a small, shining piece of beauty to history—at least to our own history, if nothing more. Once these shining moments are etched into the pages of history (even if just our own personal histories), they can never be undone.

Likewise, each moment that we use most brightly tweaks the future ever so slightly in the direction of brilliance. And within our own personal futures, perhaps the effects of not just one but a whole series of well-spent moments will alter our own timelines in an immensely positive direction.

So, we must honor and utilize the moment as best we can, now and always—whenever possible.

For when we fail to recognize the miracle of the moment, we cheat ourselves, and from a greater perspective we lengthen in some small measure the process leading up to Zenithity.

Inner Form

That which is within us, the self, may be viewed as an orb of open "space" that may be filled, moment by moment, with any number of things. Obviously, the "space" within the orb of our awareness is not literally "space," and, accordingly, it can't be measured in spatial terms. As such, the "things" that fill this orb are not physical "things" (like the types of "things" that fill up physical space), but rather are *elements* of consciousness.

This orb, our Inner Form, takes on the nature and character of the form which it assumes or possesses—the "object" of thought. This is clearly true at least to some extent, while in some respects we also remain aloof or uncolored by that which momentarily fills our Inner Form. Yet, undeniably, the contents impart some influence upon the conscious vessel. This effect upon our Inner Form can be somewhat lasting across time as well; that which colors the present may linger into the future, similarly coloring it for a while as well.

As an ideal, let us then assume those forms that are most worthy, advantageous, and phenomenal. As a guideline, we might best view the contents of our own "orbs"—not so much to see if they fit in with the expectations of our peers—but more ideally, to determine if our own Inner Form is that which is most fitting and pleasant to ourselves. This version of an individual's Inner Form would typically also be most fitting and joyful for The-All. Let's face it, beings that are mismatched with their inner surroundings typically interject an awkwardness rather than grace into the grand scheme of things.

Life is a series of interconnected experiences. Each moment is a different experience, but all moments are interconnected chronologically. The present moment is always "present" so that relatively (subjectively) the conscious orb does not move through time but merely *changes form* across time, by the moment.

There are many conditions of our experiences that we cannot change. More accurately, it is not apparent how many elements of our experience *can* be changed. Even when it is apparent that we could change some aspects of our lives, doing so may not always seem easy.

However, we do have considerable—perhaps absolute—control of the self, the vehicle by which we navigate our experiences. We are the master of this orb, our own personal "Inner Form." Accordingly, we can vastly affect the *ways* in which we experience reality. We can also choose which aspects of reality toward which we pay attention. We can also, if so motivated, change some aspects of personal, societal, and material reality to better meet our expectations.

But of more importance to our own happiness than the ability to affect reality is our ability to affect ourselves.

The Inner Forms that are most pleasing when assumed are often also those that are the most effective and vice versa: The most effective Inner Form may often yield the most pleasing states.

Absolute Truth

Absolute Truth is a conceptual notion that describes a situation wherein the absolute reality of all things is matched or understood by an exact and truthful awareness of those very same things. The Absolute Truth would be a logical, exact replica of the literal nature of Reality in all of its infinite detail and in complete totality. However, the exactly matching set of information would exist purely in consciousness, whereas the reality that it represents would exist in space, time, *and* consciousness.

Clearly, our human minds come nowhere close to comprehending the exact nature of *all* things throughout the universe, although we are remarkably adept at approximating and holding representative ideas concerning any specific thing or concept.

Beyond the extremely complex "snapshot" of Absolute Truth at any given moment in time, a more encompassing view (or version) of Absolute Truth would involve the knowledge of the exact nature of every single thing throughout the universe *as it transforms* over the eternity of time. This version of Absolute Truth, while far beyond inconceivable to the human mind, is what would be necessary to be "all knowing." The knowledge of *all* the conditions (inner and outer) of everything, large and small, as well as the position, movement, and disposition of each and every part of each and every "thing"—all of this must be known and understood (to be considered "absolute truth").

To be useful, this knowledge, though monstrously ponderous, must be understood in a moment, in the twinkling of an eye. It would not be useful if it took thousands of years to process all the parts of the information set, for by the time the reckoning finally occurred, the conditions would have changed considerably. Again, this type of all-encompassing awareness is unknown, yes, almost inconceivable to us. Yet we are, in some small measure, "conceiving" of it (or imagining the concept of it) even in this discussion.

Absolute Truth, at least in the momentary form, might be realized (in theory) by a Greater Consciousness in the far future as Consciousness might greatly and rapidly progress—as unlikely as this seems to us now. Alternately, another form of Consciousness may, on some level, possess a broad or more practical *generalized* awareness of everything. This representative awareness could constitute a "good enough" approximation of Absolute Truth.

While an understanding of the totality of Absolute Truth seems unlikely for any conscious being, it might also be unwieldly and unnecessary. Conceptualized or generalized approximations of Absolute Truth will most certainly suffice and will most likely be readily attainable by advanced forms of Life (especially when aided with information gathering, processing, and storage tools like computers).

Armed with this admittedly imperfect knowledge (the likes of which mankind has *always* contended and even more so in our humbler evolutionary origins), perhaps future advanced forms of Consciousness may somehow extrapolate or develop conceptual models of *all* the realms of all *possible* truths. Valid conceptual models of *all* possible Truths, past and future, (in addition to the current subset that fully represents the present) would constitute an approximate understanding or "roadmap" of Absolute Truth. The arrays of possible truths (possible pathways, possible futures) may be parsed and analyzed to yield an idealized subset representing an *idealized* form of Absolute Truth—such that the Absolute Truth, in the future, might match a conceptual idealized Truth as conceived by Greater Consciousness (God), or perhaps resulting in a scenario which is nearly equivalent.

Again, this is theoretical, and might occur in the early phases of Zenithity or might begin to occur in the latter phases of the Mechanysis of Perfunction. But such overarching awareness of factual tedium is *not* a necessity for the process of Zenithity to begin in earnest.

There are many pathways that lead to Zenithity, and a partial degree of knowledge of Absolute Truth, while valuable, is not necessary along most earlier pathways to the Ultimate.

The primary pathways to Zenithity can be found by any combination of dead reckoning, calculation, reason, empathy, meditative states, states unbeknownst to us, and lastly trial and error. Trial and error, an act of finding what is *better*, successively, has worked for mankind throughout history. It will presumably continue to remain effective throughout The Mechanysis of Perfunction, and can alone, if necessary, lead us (and other forms of Consciousness) to the precipice of Zenithity.

The simple action of trial and error, aided extensively by comparative hypothetical reasoning, will suffice in navigation, since the Principle of Proportionate Good will apply itself almost automatically. These simple but effective processes, aided by the more enhanced versions of our ever-evolving capabilities (briefly aforementioned), will have an accelerated rate of accuracy and resolution as we move forward.

While the old way of trial and error alone *can* be effective, any attempt to more fully understand Absolute Truth in some approximation is a worthy goal. Brilliant it would be to someday develop a "roadmap" of Absolute Truth and the underlying possibilities inherent within the future!

Gradual progress toward this corollary goal may occur in tandem along with other aspects of our advancement on the road to Zenithity. Perhaps too, our understanding of all things will accelerate wildly at some point due to factors we cannot yet imagine. While having a literal knowledge of

Absolute Truth seems far-fetched to us in the short term, we can immediately begin to strive toward a more accurate summary, or a more valid roadmap thereof. And, along the way, perhaps developing a kinder understanding of the Truth might serve us better as well.

Discovering how to navigate the pathways leading to relevant, idealized Truth sets, is of course, always a beneficial endeavor. Doing so constitutes a part of the study of Futurology—a study considerably less certain, but certainly more promising, than the study of history.

Faith in the Moment:
Truth in the Future

Lacking an absolute knowledge of Absolute Truth, some measure of faith is needed along with each measure of understanding.

Perhaps without our knowing, it is through *faith* that the bulk of our accomplishments transpire, and our existence itself subsists primarily upon wisps of subconscious faith.

Lacking the capacity to willfully animate our bodies, it is through faith alone (and forces beyond our conscious will) that we abide in each moment.

One of the greatest forms of faith is that which comes from a complete and wide-eyed willingness to accept the truth as it is, or as it will be, *whatever* that truth may be.

True faith waits patiently upon truth.

In faith, we can simply say, "I don't know everything, but I know everything will be alright."

While both wisdom and innocence may be considered virtues, wisdom is usually gained only at the expense of innocence.

Doubting the fundamental goodness of the ultimate destination is perhaps the origin of woe.

Faith is thereby the most fundamental and formidable of the known virtues.

Uncertainties Regarding Creation and God

Uncertainties of Our Past

The absolute knowledge of a creator-God is extremely difficult to ascertain. Even if somehow ascertained, it would be still more difficult to prove to many skeptically minded persons. Impossible perhaps.

In analyzing our ideas about God, we become aware that we lack the capability to *know* with any degree of certitude (from a scientific perspective) whether or not there was a "godlike" creator presiding over the origin of everything. Piecing together such a definitive knowledge would require us to assemble and examine shards and remnants of matter representing a chain of events dating back to an eternally distant moment. Any moment that seems "absolute" must have been preceded by *something* in the timeline, and any formation of matter (via clouds of particles) must have like-wise been precipitated by some other existence—for example, where did the clouds of particles come from?

It seems, therefore, that it will be nearly impossible to piece together any definitive conclusion regarding our origins from an eternally ancient position in time. The very real prospect arises that we will not likely have *any* absolute clarity of knowledge regarding whether reality was created by some form of conscious being—commonly referred to as "God."

In reflecting upon this concept, that of an initial creation occuring countless eons ago (perhaps infinitely so), we begin to know *that we cannot know* with certainty much of anything concerning our exact origins.

From this realization also arises another uniquely *freeing* perspective. We begin to become aware that this subject of creation, or more specifically, our exact personal knowledge of it, becomes somewhat less important. For the origin of everything is an event *so far removed* from our current state of existence, that the resolution of the issue within our minds may seem to be of little relevance. Life as we know it continues all the same, either way, despite the hazy cloud of uncertainty lingering over the hidden details of our primordial conception.

As we move into the future, we become aware that it is the future that matters. It is the future, and the nature of everything *within* the future, which matter more than some esoteric piece of knowledge regarding how everything originated during some nebulous event far predating the most ancient of historical times.

So, from that perspective, Zenithity provides a unique solution that encompasses or embodies the two prevalently competing notions: (1) that there is or was a creator-God and (2) that there is not or was not a creator-God. Zenithity contends, in accordance with this logical predicament regarding the factual obscurity of origins, that regardless of *how* Greater Consciousness arises (or of how consciousness has managed to exist in the first place in any way, shape, or form)—the net effect will be the same. The Greater Consciousness will emerge and coalesce in the future, regardless of the details of how it came to be in the present.

Regarding origins, there are primarily two equally unlikely possibilities. One possibility is that matter spontaneously arose from nothingness (which is theoretically impossible), and then that consciousness managed to somehow emerge from that dead matter. The other way of looking at this dilemma is to assume that consciousness existed *prior* to the existence of matter, and that this primal form of consciousness somehow "created" matter. In this second theory, matter was created or came into existence primarily as a type of meta-conscious construct. In other words, matter is, or at least was, spawned from, a form of consciousness. Then we might still ask, "Well then, if so, how did that consciousness come into being?"

It seems more likely (when comparing these two impossibly unlikely occurrences) that the second theory is slightly more plausible. That is to say, that it seems more likely that a form of consciousness existed prior to any form of "creation" (or that consciousness existed for infinity thus "predating" time and space), than it does to assume that matter would have spontaneously burst into existence or that solid (or elemental) matter would "somehow" have existed for all of the eternal past.

Still, it is not decidedly so, and there remains the possibility that all of reality is not derived from a form of conscious construct, but instead that consciousness arose as a latter-day development inside of an eternally existing universe comprised initially of dumb, lifeless matter. Either origin is equally unlikely from a logical perspective, yet here we are: consciously existing in a world in which *any* origin narrative is almost impossible to validate or prove.

While one possibility seems to appeal to some individuals, the alternative appears to be just as relevant to others. Perhaps even this is as it should be, for in a condition of uncertainty, we as a species must remain considerate and be mindful of all possibilities.

There are perhaps additional scenarios that we have not considered, but it seems that *any* theory we might propose would likewise be based so far in the antecedent as to be impossible to prove. And any theory regarding creation must uniquely satisfy the dilemma of how we get something from nothing. Using the type of reasoning with which we are endowed, it would seem that no theory of creation could ever definitively answer that riddle to the satisfaction of all reasoning beings.

But of primary importance, from the perspective of Zenithity, the exact conditions of our origin do not matter so greatly. Zenithity does not require that consciousness comes into existence in one way versus another. The net sum of the effects of Consciousness will result in the same ultimate set of future conditions. Most likely there will arise ever higher forms of consciousness, and conceivably a 'Godlike' aggregate consciousness will one day emerge.

So again, those conjectures concerning our point of origin pale in comparison to that toward which we are drawn—the future. The theories surrounding Zenithity uniquely predict that the net sum of the future is the same whether there was or was not a conscious element involved in creation. More conclusively, the net sum of consciousness, which we experientially know exists (at least in small measure), now constitutes and will culminate in (or yield) that Greater Consciousness—which might be called "God" or "The-All".

That is one of the primary premises of Zenithity, and it is viable despite our inability to *know* decisively whether or not there was a "Godlike" moment of creation. If there was or is a godlike form of consciousness in addition to the type of consciousness we know, then that godlike form of consciousness will clearly be a part—yes, clearly the most significant part— of the Greater Consciousness. And, if there was or is no such an overarching or godlike form of consciousness, then the Greater Consciousness will still be, and is, the net sum of all consciousness.

This Greater Consciousness, in its future state, is indeed quite godlike, and from there it drives and draws us forward through the rightful exercise of time.

Uncertainties of the Present

These uncertainties regarding the existence of a "God" spill over into our observations in the present. Today, there remain sharp divides concerning how to interpret the present moment with respect to the presence or absence of God.

For some, the notion of a super-conscious presence filling and enabling each moment is incontrovertible, because it seems that each moment could not be possible unless it were animated by a very deliberate act of a living God. The mere fact that we live and breathe each day shines forth with the evidence of God's order and goodness. Otherwise, everything would fragment into utter chaos; consciousness itself would not be possible as we know it.

To others, regardless of whether everything was created by a "God" in a distant act of inception, his presence seems sorely lacking from our present existence. Individual beings seem to be randomly self-directed, and there appears to be no overarching sense of "order" or "good" in this world. If God exists, where is he?

In this dilemma, without a definitively demonstrative presence of God, either of these conclusions can be understood as logically valid. Without clearly evident, irrefutable evidence of God's presence, we can easily conclude that he is not present. Unless of course, God is something other than what we normally define him to be.

But definitions and wordplay aside, there is no undeniable evidence of the existence of God, although some conclude that *everything* is, in fact, evidence of God's existence.

So, around and round we go.

Wearily, some of us step off the spinning carousel, convinced that we *must* "believe" that it is one way or the other. Without any real clarity, some of us throw all our weight behind one concept or the other—and there entrenched we remain.

The correctness of either conclusion, from the perspective of the theory of Zenithity, does not truly matter so much. Or perhaps that was stated incorrectly. *An individual's belief* (or lack thereof) concerning the existence of God (or not) does not matter so much. God, if he exists, does so regardless of the opinions or beliefs of individuals.

Another reason to assume that it is safe to conclude that our opinions regarding the existence (or not) of God do not matter so very much is that there is no overwhelmingly obvious observability of God. Another way to query and conclude this is; *if* God exists, and *if* he is an "all-powerful" God, then *if* he wanted you to absolutely believe in his existence, then he would make his existence *indisputably* obvious. In making his presence undeniable, there might be billboards in the sky, and personal visits with handshakes, and so on. There would be no lack of clarity, no "dilemma," if it were so important to God, for us to "believe" in him.

Also, if God truly wanted everyone to believe in his existence, he would probably prohibit us from making doubtful statements of this type or even thinking in this way. If it were vital for the created to believe in their creator, then such beliefs would be obligatory and automatic.

So, one might easily conclude that because God did not make his existence obviously and irrefutably apparent, there can be no God. But again, this assumes that God must meet certain requirements that we humans have solely devised.

Let's restate the original dilemma to see if there are different conclusions that *could* possibly support the notion of a God.

If God exists, and *if* he is an "all-powerful" God, then *if* he wanted you to absolutely believe in his existence, then he would make his existence indisputably obvious. But maybe there are too many "ifs." Maybe the Almighty is not *all* powerful, at least not in the way that *we* perceive. Perhaps he can spin matter into existence from low-level conscious constructs and perhaps he can sub-animate discrete moments of time, but perhaps he does not have a physical body with which to shake hands. More importantly, perhaps he does not have emotions of the type that require him to *want* you to "believe" in him.

Philosophically we might search for a set of conditions that would explain this apparent contradiction – the existence of a God who makes his existence unapparent, unobvious, or obfuscated. In constructing conditions that logically support this apparent contradiction, we might conclude many of our stacked conditional arguments with the phrase, "and if he *wanted* you to believe in him." But in the most logical explanation, perhaps that entire "if clause" does not exist. Perhaps—and please don't take this personally— perhaps God, as evidenced by his un-obviousness does not *care* whether you believe in him or not?

To take this one step further, perhaps there is a type of fundamental consciousness that exists, which could be called God in some contexts. And perhaps that fundamental type of consciousness is so different from what we can imagine that it does not care if we believe or not. In fact, perhaps God exists, but does not really even have the capacity to care (or not care) whether we believe. In other words, the type of ego-based self-concern, which we might feel if someone didn't believe in us, is not even a possibility for "God."

Let us reflect and step outside the box a little more and back track to our discussion of conscious *origins*. It appears as if the conscious-based origins may be more likely in our reflections and observations as discussed regarding those past possibilities. It simply seems more improbable that everything would just "happen" without consciousness. It seems most unlikely that physical matter (or physical energy) would just spontaneously come into existence. But when we examine the *current* dilemma from a purely logical perspective, it seems a little more likely—due to a lack of any obvious demonstrative evidence—that a God does *not presently* exist. And while I know that our conjecture on any topic of this nature is vague at best, this is a conclusion which I am not happy to admit.

But in both dilemma-laden scenarios, past and present, it is perhaps our notions of what God *might be* that are lacking. In considering both past and present scenarios *together*, the most likely alternative may be that a primitive form of consciousness both originated matter as a form of conscious construct, and fundamentally animates (in the present) some aspects of that matter as it progresses endlessly through a series of events across moments in time. The lack of obviousness attributable to this underlying conscious matrix (the likely present form of "God") might be explained by the idea that this form of consciousness is of a type that has no need or means to conspicuously advertise or prove itself in any capacity.

The existence of other explanations beyond our own current capacity to understand might also be in play here. But in our attempts to understand, we wish to assert and aim to elucidate those which appear to be the most plausible explanations.

Alas, for all of this conjecture, as important as it seems, the relevance may be rather diminished in comparison with that state within which Consciousness resides in the future. The direction toward which all things are drawn is the driving force that gives meaning and purpose into each present moment. Each present moment spills fluidly over into the future, and in that direction all conscious entities of *all* types are invested.

Fully actualized in that future,
we will find the cumulative best of our conscious endeavors.

Perhaps there too we will realize an expanded understanding of all that remains elusive today. For in the future, the gravity of these dilemmas will abate, as the dilemmas themselves will be resolved.

The Way of the Future

Everything occurring within the past is but history, and the further in the past that an event lies, the less bearing it has upon the present. The further in the past any moment resides, the less clarity we have in evaluating it. And isn't the conceptual instant of creation hidden away in an indeterminately distant past? If so, should that unknowable event be so distracting to us as to cloud our judgment of the present or to blur our progress into the future?

History is a valuable study. Not only is it quite interesting, but it is a discipline wherein we may learn something of ourselves. We learn about what mistakes were made, and conversely, we can reflect upon what was done right, that is, which actions and events advanced the human condition.

In looking at history in this way and reflecting on the past, we understand that history teaches us how to better live in the present and how to use the present to more effectively influence our futures.

In the context of history, we can include our own personal histories. Anything in the past constitutes some part of history. For us as individuals, the recollections of events and experiences that were personally important to us are the more relevant parts of history.

Through our awareness of our own past mistakes and triumphs, we can not only savor those thoughts, but we can better adapt to the present. Finally, by reviewing our past experiences, we can be better prepared for the future, or stated more positively, we can prepare for a better future.

So, while the study of history and the review of our personal past experiences are important tools that we have at our disposal, they may be over emphasized. Futurology, the study of the future, is perhaps a more fitting and fruitful pursuit. It is our orientation toward the future that effectuates the greatest amount of influence. We should never forget the important lessons of the future, nor should we allow the future to be confined by our limited understandings of the past.

Via Futurology, we deliberately focus at least *some* of our energies forward—in the direction we are traveling. Just as when driving, we must keep our eyes on the road, and our attention focused generally ahead. The rearview mirror receives only an occasional glance. Our navigational map shows where we are going and the routes we may take. A map showing only places that we have already been, is little more than a showpiece, a novelty, or a souvenir.

With Futurology, while *living* most fully in the present and *learning* from the past, we become more adept at navigating possible outcomes. We can live in a future-forward state of mind where the possibilities become more important than the unchangeable events and relics of the past.

The origin stories concerning how "everything" arose, while interesting and perhaps having some influence and historical importance, are an ever-distant, and ever-fading topic. And clearly, in our present, it is not the intention of "God" (if he exists in the manner that we would suppose) to have us affixed only on his presence and on his presence alone. Clearly too, reality exists currently in such a manner that:

We are free, almost encouraged by the very nature of reality, to pursue our lives in the best ways forward that we can conceive,

and we must do so in the absence of any clearly obvious guideposts or guardrails.

So, enough with the over-concern regarding "God" and origins. Let us move, right-facing, into the future—and facing more rightly into the future. Therein is the "will" of God as I see it: that we should stand upright and tall in the present moment, enjoying and honoring all of Life, which he has miraculously provided. In the absence of any obvious or compelling directives to the contrary, it seems to be his will that we should forge ahead *in our own ways* of making our own best possible futures.

His will is thus fulfilled and satisfied by our highest and best endeavors:

This way will ultimately become '*His*' way.

By successively following and progressing through all that is best,

We find our rightful destiny.

This is the Way of the Future.

A Healthy Dose of Skepticism

In any of the endeavors we follow in life, and especially regarding philosophies or ideals, a good amount of skepticism is warranted. It is skepticism that keeps us from falling astray, or worse, falling into great pits of misery. Skepticism is one of our most useful tools in this world, and it should not be dispensed with lightly.

Furthermore, skepticism may be said to fall *generally* into one of two categories:

Caring Skepticism – This is skepticism that is generally helpful, not in that it is necessarily always correct, but in that it comes from a place of caring. Only by caring about the outcome is this kind of skepticism possible. It is a skepticism that says, "I care about the outcome, so I want to make sure we do not make this or that mistake or miscalculation.

So, I am offering my heartfelt *criticism* so that we might improve the outcome." It is born of caring and is therefore always valid for consideration. A rational mind, after considering the skeptic's well-founded concerns over the welfare of the operation or the individuals involved, may weigh the pros and cons, reflect on all conceivable ramifications, and then decide upon a course rationally. Thus the skeptics concerns, if they were valid, may have mitigated or improved the outcomes.

Disruptive Skepticism - This skepticism may sound the same, and may even echo the same sentiments as those originating from a place of caring, but the source and the intent are different. Some people have, for any number of reasons, a generalized sense of malcontent. From this generalized malcontent can arise a rather dark skepticism that is without any good intent. These personality types project a negative skepticism onto almost everything they contact.

Such skepticism says, "I am unhappy and unsuccessful, and I want to make sure everyone else remains the same way. So, I will rain derision down upon any attempt at lightness, empowerment, or betterment."

For observers, distinguishing the source or tone of the skepticism may be difficult—and often may not matter. Regardless of source or apparent tone, the facts regarding any skepticism should be considered in a rational and caring manner.

Additionally, when we, as individuals, are the source of skepticism, we should be wary and introspective, making sure not only that our concerns are well founded, but also that what drives our hesitancy is coming from a good and genuine place. We must guard against malicious or ill-willed derision.

That said, skepticism is a critical part of The Mechanysis of Perfunction and the path to Zenithity. It is both part of the process and inherently becomes a part of the solution. Clearly, none of us knows today what is "ideal" or "best." While we must iteratively navigate toward that which is "better" and do so with reasonable vigor and energy, we must also proceed with some caution and with the guidance that is sometimes provided in the form of skepticism.

Concerning this (and any) important process, or any of the details found therein, the following applies:

It is best to have a healthy dose of skepticism toward the details along any chosen path, a skepticism tempered with a healthy dose of enthusiasm regarding the overall journey and its outcome.

Furthermore, a great deal of skepticism is warranted before embarking upon any chosen path or journey, as a foreboding set of circumstances may warrant choosing another path, or taking none whatsoever until conditions warrant. As the old saying goes, "An ounce of prevention is worth a pound of cure."

So, again, skepticism regarding these ideas and philosophies is welcome, and even encouraged. For the best ideas and ideals are those that can withstand a rigorous degree of cross-examination and questioning. As the saying goes, "The hardest steel is forged by the hottest flame."

The ideas which prevail will be the most immediately advantageous and useful in the here and now—the ideas that "advance the ball" the farthest, in the shortest period of time. And in the end, those will be (or lead us to) the ideas and ideals that withstand the tests of time.

Admittedly, this theory, this philosophy, is prone to error, as are all philosophies and theories. But bear in mind the following guideline in adjudicating all imperfect matters of this nature:

The best ideas are those which best serve Life.

Be the most skeptical of those ideas which detract from Life.

Science and Beyond

Among the forms of skepticism, previously noted and generally lauded, there are two that are often intractable, and these seem to have spewed forth from the belly of abject stubbornness.

These are:

Literalism/Scripturalism—This is a persistent belief system containing a rigidity based upon the printed words of ancient beings (humans), which are typically related to religious notions passed down by our primitive forbearers. While these rigid beliefs were originally oriented specifically toward cultural/historical/religious topics, they now seem to have spilled over into all areas of thought and conjecture. Within these mindsets dwells an unwillingness to accept any idea that does not coincide with a given person's interpretation of a literal piece of ancient doctrine—regardless of how fantastical or illogical that ancient tale or diatribe may be.

Scientism—In modern times, the degree of stubbornness arising from those who think they know everything because they have read a science book or two is at times bewildering. They may have become more recalcitrant than the scripturalist. It seems they can stamp any view they wish as "scientific" and thereby deny all other reasonable conclusions, thus assuming "supreme indisputable authority" regarding any viewpoint so stamped. This trend is more befuddling and disconcerting than the obfuscating illusions of the religious literalist; that persons who are presumably "thinkers" would wish to abdicate that role in favor of simply assigning the title of "scientific" to any hastily drawn conclusion that they wish to favor.

It is the latter that we discuss here, and the scripturalists will be addressed later.

The Flaws of Intractable Scientism

Science is a method. More accurately, it has become a term that encompasses several fields of study that loosely follow a certain method known, surprisingly enough, as the *scientific method.*

The scientific method is nothing more than a generalized recipe for proving or validating a set of ideas concerning a specific subject or phenomenon. Key to the scientific method is the notion of developing a set of well-reasoned, reproducible methods in order to test a hypothesis. If the set of conditions in the "experiment" are well reasoned, and can demonstrate a cause-and-effect relationship (while ruling out other potentially intervening factors), then we may say that the experiment is "scientific" and that it meets the criteria of the scientific method. Then, any other persons performing the same reproducible experiment will produce either an effect that verifies the initial hypothesis or results that deny or refute the original hypothesis. Perhaps most importantly, the experiment, if repeated multiple times, and even if repeated reliably by other individuals, should yield the same result regarding the original hypothesis.

What we now call "science," a broad field of studies based loosely upon the scientific method, has indeed yielded many advancements we enjoy daily (and perhaps we take many of these advancements for granted). We live in a world that is largely formatted, supported, and enhanced by thousands of achievements in the various fields of science. In almost every aspect of life, science (and technology, clearly an extension of science) has conquered many of the serious problems and ills that were prevalent in the lives of our ancestors. The workings of the modern world, with its massive population and advanced societies, are not possible without the myriad of major and minor advancements formerly contributed by scientists, inventors, and engineers. The results of these multilayered scientific advancements are interwoven into nearly every aspect of our lives, creating the comfortable and fulfilling way of life most of us now enjoy. Most of us, without these scientific advancements, would perish or find ourselves miserably embroiled in one bitter struggle for survival after another. To be fair, science (rather than religion), has "saved us" from so many of our problems. Hardworking and logical people of science, not the pompous kings and priests, have uplifted us from the pits of poverty, disease, and constant struggle.

Sure, some will deny this, believing that, on the contrary, science is responsible for all the problems facing the modern world rather than for the solutions. Indeed, sometimes it seems that for every solution developed by science there is a downside, or an unwanted side effect. To some people, the side effect is now seen as more troublesome than the original problem. Perhaps this is because many of us have been born in an era wherein the 'old problems' (like starvation) no longer exist, so we see only the negative side effects of the science which conquered starvation (like algae blooms from fertilizer usage, and concerns over preservatives in food).

It is important that we put it all into proper perspective and understand that the initial problems were often *far* greater than the newer problems (or side effects). In general, progress has been made via science across the board. Certainly, the naysayers are right to question the side effects, and the downsides—not to do away entirely with the initial solutions, but rather to improve upon them, or perhaps to find even better alternatives. As we progress through seemingly stratified layers of problems, typically working upward from the more significant issues first, the goal is to resolve each new layer of problems while ideally creating solutions with as few unwanted side effects as possible.

In this light, science is a vital and highly welcome part of the process leading to Zenithity. Science has conquered more problems facing mankind in the last 500 years than did our superstitions in the previous 50,000 years. And certainly, if some people wish to live in a world without science (or the resulting technologies), then perhaps some primitive island can exist for them. There they can have a taste of those ancient lifestyles before they quickly come running (and screaming) back to the modern world—that is, if they are lucky enough (and strong enough, mentally and physically) to survive.

Again, it is difficult to imagine a world in which progress is valued without imagining science running in tandem with the progress in every facet and manner possible.

So, one might ask, "What then, exactly is the problem, with science?"

Well, there is no problem with science. As mentioned, science is nothing but a methodology. As such, science has no emotions. Science has no sentiments. Science has no feelings. Science has no obstinacy. Science has no opinion. Science especially has no valid opinion on anything which it can't measure or quantify.

So, the problem is not with science. It is difficult to have any problem with the above stated facts. The problem lies within some people's attachment to their own particular notion of science, or to what they believe to be science. It is their attaching the label and trappings of science to their pet ideas for which often no valid basis exists. This tendency, often exuded from the minds of some relatively learned men, becomes a stubbornness and a lack of insightfulness that rivals the blind purveyors of any religion from the darkest of ages.

Fanatics armed with their "belief" in "science" (or something they believe or perceive to be "scientific") will shun all reason, all light, and all opinion but their own. Their attitude seems to be: In the name of science, may you all be damned.

Along with their rigid beliefs they are charged with emotion, sentiment, feelings, obstinacy, and mostly—cloaked within and clearly labeled as "science"—there lie voluminous piles of unbridled and often falsified opinions.

Science, lest we forget, is but a *branch* of reason and logic, and not the other way around. Reason and logic are still necessary to develop hypotheses, construct valid experiments, and especially to *objectively evaluate* the results. The use of the conscious attribute of reasoning is *always* applied to any observation or evaluation that is considered scientific, yet among the adherents of scientism, all other forms of reasoning are demonized, as is the "father" of science, *reason itself.*

Could we possibly develop an experiment to test many of the theories advanced within this treatise? Certainly not. Only our unique capacities for reasoning can guide us in these and many other important matters. If we are to exclude every manner of thought and every reasonable conclusion, merely because it does not fit some schoolboy notion of a science experiment, then we are to wander off into the abyss of a trite and trivial void of meaninglessness.

The problem is not so much that people are eager to use science properly, but that they are too eager to jump to false conclusions irrationally. Then they cleverly brandish the words "scientific" or "science" as if that somehow prohibits any further discussion or analysis. In truth, the attitude against questioning or analysis is very *anti-scientific.*

Scientism has ironically become the antithesis to true science.

A False Sense of Security

Another issue sometimes arises in our modern world dominated by science and technology. We are surrounded by such complexity and technology that tends to all of societies necessities. Often unseen and unknown by the individual, this abstract bundle of complexity usually "works as intended," so we have no choice but to blindly accept all of it. After all, there is no way that any individual could really understand *all* of the technology that surrounds us. Such a task would be much too daunting. We can use a computer, drive a car, and have laser surgery performed on our eyes, but a typical individual would most likely never fully understand the inner workings of all of these diversified "miracles" of technology. For example, most of us could never build a car from scratch, much less, even repair one if handed the necessary parts.

So, sometimes, we make no effort to understand, and that is certainly understandable. We have no intention of, nor any need for, understanding *everything*. But in accepting *so much* of that which comprises our day-to-day environment, without any reflection, we can begin to habitually accept *all* things rather blindly. We occupy a world in which we may feel diminished, seemingly overshadowed at times by the technology that surrounds us. This too is not so wrong or bad, in and of itself. But the way of thinking that it generates may be lacking in any critical thought or scientific objectivism. It is ironic that as we become overshadowed by the technological innovations of science, we begin to lose, by sheer weight of information overload, the skeptical objectivity that is most essential to science.

Perhaps this is all dancing about a finer point, which is; by developing a thought pattern of "accepting" any scientific or technological innovation simply "because it seems to work," we have perhaps developed a corollary thought pattern of accepting any notion that is espoused as scientific. Some of us have become too weary to do the legwork and apply critical thought to the very important issues facing us. Since we begin to feel as if "everything is being handled" by nameless others who are presumably more technically and intellectually adept, we begin to stop utilizing reason and the other finer faculties of the mind. In the comfortable nest provided by an "all-knowing" science, we often fail to reflect and apply thought concerning inner and outer matters which actually matter. It seems, at times, that we have stopped thinking.

In this way, there is a dual nature regarding the growing rigidity of the mindset of scientism:

The hubris of the "all-knowing" elites of science, who espouse certainty over topics which they clearly do not fathom, is reciprocated by growing numbers of ordinary people who have dismissed or 'shrugged off' their innate conscious responsibilities of using reflection and reason in daily matters as well as in deeper matters of importance.

Perhaps it is just 'nicer', more comfortable, or safer to assume that everything is known than to assume that perhaps a great deal is not known.

But lurking behind the false confidence and mental laziness affecting both faces of scientism, are a series of holes. Great holes exist in the body of knowledge that we often perceive as quite complete. Some would say the holes are larger than the actual substance of the known, and some take this further and state that all which we know is *entirely surrounded* by holes. The reality of our amassed understanding can be more succinctly portrayed:

The known is bounded on all sides by the unknown.

Holes Surrounding Knowledge

If we delve very deeply in any direction, we will discover the unknown on the fringes of the known. On all fronts, we will find that all of our suppositions and assumptions are bounded by that which is unknown. The known can be visualized as a ball floating in a sea of the unknown.

> *The basis, or the foundation of the known,*
> *can be found unattached, and untethered,*
> *dangling precariously into the unknown.*

If this still seems rather nebulous, let's consider a few examples.

Consider time, a topic we have discussed quite a bit.

What does science tell us of time?

Not much really. Science measures almost every possible result of every possible experiment using time. A particular chemical evaporates at some number of milliliters per hour. An hour, in this equation, represents the passage of a certain amount of time. The velocity of a rocket is 10,000 feet per second. The second is a segment of time: a fairly reliable measurement of a quick period of time, one 60th of a minute to be less precise. Time is vital to the understanding of nearly every scientific experiment or observation.

But just because we *use* time in every calculation to somehow quantify every change, we have yet to adequately define time itself.

Perhaps we should ask the scientist,
"What exactly is this thing (time) that you are dividing into another thing, as in miles/hour? Certainly, you have measured time, or durations of time (using clocks or other time-measuring apparatuses). But simply because you have accurately measured something does not mean that you understand it or know what it is, or why it exists, or how it is perpetuated. We have not even begun to explore the finer characteristics or qualities of this essence we call time; we have only measured it quite linearly. We can measure a person's height as he stands against the wall, but that tells us very little about that person, or about people in general."

So, we ask scientists, "Exactly what is time?" Well, they can't really define it adequately. Even though they refer to it in every calculation, observation, and experiment, they really do not know exactly what it is.

"Why is time here?"

This also they do not know.

"*When* will you know what time is, exactly?"

The scientist must admit, "We probably will not be able to tell you *exactly* what time is, not any time soon, because we can't come up with any experiments to determine what it is. Almost every experiment uses time, and a voluminous body of results are expressed in units of time, but we can't quantify or adequately explain what time *is*. We simply fall back to that admittedly unscientific conclusion that people just innately *know* what time *is*. It's just common knowledge. It's common sense."

Common sense.

So, nearly every aspect of science is based upon our 'personal awareness' of what time 'is.' Yet basing anything on 'personal awareness' or 'common sense' is a cardinal sin within science. In philosophy we must often rely upon the fact that some things are inherently known by people, and sometimes these can't be, or need not be, demonstrated any further. When philosophers do this, it is considered unscientific. If scientists do the same thing, then it is OK and it can even form the foundation of every branch of their science.

For the philosopher resides in a unique form of hell, to which the scientist does not yet realize that he also belongs. To the philosopher, the greatest fear is, "What if I am wrong?" And in many ways, he most certainly is.

It would be better to internally and personally consider well-reasoned ideas concerning the nature of time (and consciousness) than to ask a person hard-tacked to the rigid rigors of science. Their answer will lack creativity and insight, since they long since abandoned these finer qualities to rote analytical observation alone.

There is a real issue with being pedantic concerning which methods one may use to come to valid conclusions. Especially when lacking the capacity to perform observable science concerning certain topics (time or consciousness, for example), one must resort to that aspect of Consciousness from which science itself was also born: sheer reasoning.

Sadly, sheer reasoning may be becoming a lost art. This is partly due to overly relying on the science of observability and on an educational system intent on teaching people only how to be taught instead of how to think. We seem to have forgotten to encourage people to think, and to think reasonably yet creatively.

Another example of a glaring uncertainty within science is our understanding of gravity, which has been around longer than we have. But scientists still have not defined it nor do they know why it exists. However, the concept of gravity exists in nearly every calculation within astrophysics and other disciplines. The not so bright will say, "Oh, well, they have measured the rate of fall of an apple, and a piece of bacon, and found that they are the same. And they have measured the speed, or rather the acceleration caused by gravity. Good enough. We certainly know it all now."

Bravo. This is truly great. We have been able to measure and quantify the effects of something so commonplace as gravity. We can measure the acceleration due to gravity according to how quickly something falls over a period of time.

It is ironic, that one undefinable fundamental, gravity, is measured almost solely in terms of another undefinable fundamental, time.

But *actually* what *is* gravity? Why does gravity do what it does? Why does it exist? They don't really know. Why did gravity come into existence in the first place, and why does it continue to exist?

Here's a clue; they really don't know.

They do know gravity goes along with matter; the more matter, the more gravity. They can even devise formulas on the mass of matter and the corresponding amount of gravity. So, gravity is associated with matter, but that does not explain what it is or why it exists and persists. It doesn't begin to explain *how* it works.

Identifying that one thing is obviously associated with another is not really definitive; in recognizing certain relationships in this way we have not truly defined either party in the relationship.

Again, this is not meant to deride this achievement, for understanding the relationship between mass and gravity is a truly amazing accomplishment. But being able to attach numbers to something is not the same as understanding that thing.

The best of our scientists simply do not understand what *causes* gravity. They can measure or predict the amount of gravity (or pull) that exists between any two masses, but they can't describe *why* that force exists in the first place nor why the "pull" that gravity exerts occurs. They have simply made verifiable observations that this pull does, in fact, occur.

In the case of gravity and so many fundamental aspects of our universe, we believe that we know so much because we can measure some of these, in some manner. In actuality, we really know so little.

At best our scientists have attached numbers to further describe an event like gravity that we already understand on one very fundamental and personal level. Amazingly the numbers do help regarding quantification. But science did not make the phenomenon, nor does it fully understand it. Science does not own the universe, nor the knowledge of it.

Did scientists create gravity? Sometimes it seems as though they would like you to *believe* they did. But they do not *own* gravity. They do not even understand how or why gravity exists. They have really only *measured* it.

They can produce numbers that describe or define a thing further, and often these definitions are themselves expressed in terms of other things (like time) which, in turn, we do not really understand.

These are but a few examples, and they are probably not even the very best examples. But one can easily explore the validity of the notion that we are bounded (or surrounded) on all sides by the unknown. It can be easily demonstrated, that if we ask enough valid questions (about eight) in any direction regarding anything, we will without fail encounter the unknown. This occurs in every direction, and as such the underpinnings of our knowledge are anchored and tethered within the unknown.

The edges of the void in which our knowledge exists can be found fewer than 8 steps away in any direction.

Jayce's Conundrum

Our knowledge is founded upon, bounded on all sides, and surrounded by, the unknown.

To test this premise is quite simple:

1. Start with any "factual" (preferably scientific) statement or piece of knowledge.
2. Ask a valid probing question expressing a fundamental uncertainty regarding the "factual" statement.
3. Provide the best-known answer to the question.
4. Fundamentally question the previous answer.
5. Repeat steps 3 and 4, six more times or until the question can't be answered with certainty.
6. Congratulations! You have found one of the outer edges or boundaries of knowledge!
7. If not, try improving your question making skills.

Science as a Tool among Tools

In conclusion, science—true science—may in fact form the backbone or musculature of the process of Zenithity. Or maybe not. But it is equally important to note that some understandings will certainly come in an altogether different form. We have made tremendous progress with math-based science and engineering, but now we are under the charm or spell of believing that all things can be understood *only* through math and experimental observational science.

These are the types of unyielding conundrums we face when envisioning the world only with entrenched, opinionated scientism. But the rigidity of this equation too will change.

Lastly, as a side note, concerning time, as in the former example; the true understanding of time will most likely come in a form of consciousness we have not yet fully developed. This form of understanding will most likely be a form of reasoning that lies beyond math and science.

And that too is a theory, like so many other theories, which at this juncture, we can neither prove nor disprove via any means available to science.

Only time will tell.

Religions of Old and God of the New

When we speak of "old religions," we are typically referring to those that are no longer considered "active" or perhaps are only active in the sense that there is a "retro" or revived sense of superficial interest in them. For example, there is currently a modern revival of interest in historical customs and beliefs of early European pagan origins. As these were the beliefs of some of our ancient forebears, there is some value in acknowledging those teachings and their influence on mankind's early advancement.

At a latter point in time the old religions became more commonly described as "mythologies." These religions, now largely considered mere legend and lore, include the polytheistic religions of the ancient Greeks, Romans, and the Norse Mythologies. We are familiar with the tales of Odin, Zeus, Thor, Loki, and Apollo—to name a few. Notably, there were also female deities in those ancient religions—Aphrodite, Venus, Hera, and Diana, for example. The tales of these ancient but perhaps forgotten 'deities' still fill the pages of many books.

Those same tales once influenced human history, and made some impact on our development, presumably for the positive. Whether the stories are literally true or not is beside the point. The point is, the lessons and morals *gleaned* from those tales held some sway over people during those earlier times. The stories played some role in the development of the budding civilizations during that era. The notions contained within those stories helped or guided people at that stage of human development as they rose from a more primitive state to a (slightly more) civilized state.

For *our* purposes, in discussing 'old religions', we might also consider the primary religions prevalent within society today. Let's face it: today's religions were mostly established or codified 1,000 or more years ago.

It could be said that several of our present-day religions and some of their teachings, were *once* quite ahead of their times. At the time they were first established, the teachings of Christianity (now over two thousand years old), could be said to be perhaps five hundred years ahead of their time. This is one of the reasons Christianity was adopted in earlier eras (in many regions) despite the open persecution of Christians (or anyone who challenged the local 'pagan' priesthoods). Who knows, perhaps those teachings were even *1,000 years* ahead of their time. But were all of those teachings, parables, and stories, ahead of their time by 2,000 years?

Certainly, some of the beliefs of Christianity were crucial for advancing the human species beyond a fairly entrenched set of rigid viewpoints that were quite limiting. For example, before the time of Christ, most people in every culture believed that some form of blood sacrifice—animal and sometimes human—was needed to 'appease' the gods. This belief was incredibly prevalent throughout the world, although today we probably find it illogical and even revolting.

Was this a *healthy* set of rituals to be performed repeatedly around the world? Did the pointless killing of a random poor animal (or person) really appease the gods and bring rain to help grow the crops? I think not; if it were so, then we are living in the *stupidest* universe possible.

Now we can see that such rituals and beliefs were not only distractingly futile and cruel but were clearly counterproductive. Such suffering and loss. Such a colossal diversion from the real issues. Primitive people, if they had not been so entrenched in their ritualistic beliefs, would have been much better served by studying agriculture and enacting works of irrigation to 'help make the crops grow' instead of mindlessly engaging in superstitious sacrifices to appease nonexistent and very "angry gods."

It took the Lamb of God to begin leading the world out of this tragic and very limiting mindset. We often take this fundamental advancement offered by early Christianity for granted.

In his words, deeds, and the example of his personal story, Jesus demonstrated that God's forgiveness is universal, not derived from our works and especially not from some hollow blood ritual.

He paid the ultimate sacrifice to get this simple point across to a species that was entrenched and entranced by ancient teachings that were of little or no relevance. Religious practices and teachings that were once pillars of wisdom, had become stumbling blocks of ignorance. Beliefs that are both false and yet rigidly insistent can become a great hindrance and can even have quite a decidedly harmful effect upon people spanning centuries of time. Unburdening ourselves from this heavy yoke has historically been proven to be quite difficult.

Many other teachings offered by Christianity, as espoused primarily by Jesus or Paul, are of considerable and perhaps never-ending value. This is an amazing legacy; to have remained valid after 2000 years. And many of these teachings were rooted in ancient Jewish teachings reaching back a few millennia prior. Talk about standing the test of time! We can clearly see that several of the teachings of Christianity, and the other 'old religions,' are indeed eternally sublime. They have real value for us today and will continue to have value as far as can be seen.

While one may find countless valuable teachings within Christianity, there are a few that are truly outstanding and fundamental. The Golden Rule, for instance, states simply: Treat others as *you* would like to be treated.

Or perhaps stated differently: Do not do anything to others that you know would be harmful to them.

Another key teaching arising from Christianity is that of salvation by grace. This is the belief that we are saved from "sin" (the errors of our ways), not via our own works, but by the sheer grace of God, who having created all things, assumes responsibility (symbolically through the Messiah's great sacrifice) for *all* the sins and errors of all creation.

The values still strongly standing, which are offered by Christianity (and other 'current' old religions) are numerous; certainly none of them are to be forgotten or lightly dismissed. The great challenges facing humanity in the past were often overcome, at least in part, due to our ancestors' faith in these principles and due to our observances of some of the timeless morals imparted by the teachings. It is frightening to imagine what *might have become*, if *none* of these morals had existed, or if there were no faith, and no uplifting principles. We would most likely have been a doomed and barbaric species, living in catastrophically failed societies—that is, if we had continued to survive at all.

But, by characterizing these religions as "old," we acknowledge that there are some aspects within them that seem *outdated*, some parts that seem counterintuitive and perhaps even counterproductive. Some of the curiously irrational trappings of the old religions may actually repel potential adherents from the finer and nobler sentiments which have real value.

First and foremost, many modern-day followers of these religions prescribe a type of literalism or scripturalism wherein one must 'believe' in *all* of their texts, not just those parts that have relevance or clarity. These "followers" will interject their rigid beliefs, based upon their interpretations of these ancient scripts, into *every* discussion concerning every possible outcome. And when the logical preponderance of reason, logic, and benevolence contradicts their beliefs, they will always assert that their scripture is more relevant than any other facts.

We might ask in each discussion, "Well, how do you know these scripts should take absolute precedence over every other fact?"

They will answer, "Because God wrote (or inspired) these scripts."

And when we ask, "How do you know?"

They will answer, "Because the scripts said so."

This frustratingly circular illogic does not need to be interjected into *every* rational discussion. A person certainly has a right to believe as they choose, as long as they are not forcing their ideas upon others. But when scripturalism clearly lacks validity or reasonability, its constant reassertion into every topic (based every time on the underlying circular illogic and nothing more) only serves to weaken the appeal of that belief system among potential adherents.

Therein the great tragedy lies: a rejection of the finer and nobler values of a particular faith due to the incalcitrant insistence upon absolute belief in details regarding ancient stories that were (often) clearly intended as symbolic fable or parable.

For instance, we are told that we must "believe" that God destroyed a tower that was being constructed by ancient men who were cooperating across civilizations and peoples. The ancients were supposedly building the tower to try to get closer to God in the heavens above. In destroying this "tower" God *angrily* decreed that men (his creation) should speak separate languages to keep them apart. Is this a story we *must* literally believe, in order to accept the other, clearly *better* values held within the teachings of old religions?

Perhaps not.

Did a holy man turn water into wine? Did he or another turn a staff into a snake? Many of us have seen a magician do this, but it was only a trick. Perhaps he did, and perhaps he didn't. None of us were there, so to insist that it is a *known* fact is a bit disingenuous at the very least. To advance these stories as absolute fact can be seen as highly deceptive at its worst. Either way, whether or not these stories literally occurred becomes a moot point. Furthermore, it smacks of deceptiveness to claim that one *knows* with *certainty* that something *is so*, or even that something *is not so*, when one was not a party or witness to the fabled event in question. The main point here is, that the parable taught a lesson, which was perhaps useful at the time. But it is the lesson, not the story, that possibly remains useful to us today.

Beyond the teachings, meanings, principles, and morals, are we required to believe in the literality of various ancient occurrences, many of which on the surface seem quite fantastical? Must we be forced to believe in that which seems unbelievable? Is this a cruel game imposed by a God angered, yet again, by his own creation and creatures?

Certainly many of our principles, beliefs, and morals are founded upon teachings derived from ancient religions, and perhaps rightly so. Whether these ancient stories are literally accurate is not the relevant point. The *point* is that, like it or not, they are the vehicle through which many of our valuable principles and morals arrived; as such, they should be respected in some measure.

But it is these valid principles, morals, and values themselves that should furthermore be observed, honored and followed—unless there is an enlightened reason to do otherwise. It was the principles behind the stories, and not the stories themselves, that were often most relevant. The principles were the intended message, and the stories were often but a vehicle for delivering those messages in a more interesting way.

Great bedtime storytellers were the ancient sages.

The stories, if it seems they are but fairy tales, need not be "believed" literally or with great forced tenacity.

It is time that we move forward
from the fairy tales of antiquity.
Concerning our beliefs;
We must begin to remove the wheat (truths)
from the chaff (clutter)

Ideally, we should indeed keep an eye to the future, and as a result, here in the present may we hope that new and relevant teachings will arise that are themselves 500 or 1,000 years more advanced. We need teachings that are 500 or 1,000 years ahead of their times, *right now, today*. We need solid ideas and advanced ideals that build, now, on the morals and principles that we have painstakingly acquired over the last 4,000 years.

This work, this treatise, is not intended as a great, new teaching (in and of itself) that is 'vastly far ahead of its time.' Instead, this work *portends* those greater teachings which *will* arise. It encourages and urges those great teachings and ideals of the future to **come forth**. It urges those who have the light within their souls, to be unafraid, come forth, and shine!

Yes, I do not doubt that those greater teachings *will* come—and they will advance the cause of humanity, of Life, of Consciousness—perhaps 1,000 years accelerated into the future.

And then one day, maybe another 2000 years hence, perhaps today's teachings too will be replaced or sidelined as "mythology" or "old religion." But it is not for naught. For the principles and advancements, that emerge when we set our path toward a viable future that is brighter than today, are not fully lost when they are superseded by yet a newer and bolder set of ideals.

For often our newer ideals are but standing on the shoulders of giants from an earlier and more challenging era.

The gradual unveiling of truth should not be stymied by occluded musings from past eras.

So, let us not be afraid of the new, and now, let us *let the new come forth*.

For God is *said* to have said, in his favorite proclamation:

"Behold, I am doing a new thing!"

And, just what does that imply?

Do we suppose, in our own sleepy and provincial corners of the world, that there can and will be *no new things*?

So, let us facilitate, and not become impediments *to*, his great unfurling process.

For God was, and is, and always will be, a God of the new.

He is, after all:

The Master of the New

Dialogues across Types of Consciousness

Of consciousnesses, we are a type, a very specific type derived from a generalized super set of consciousnesses. We might easily conclude that there are potentially other types of consciousness, some more fundamental, some more advanced, and others altogether quite different. There may be entire types of consciousness, the likes of which we may not yet have encountered or conceived.

God, for example, can be imagined as an infinite pool of the most fundamental or elemental type of consciousness. As such, all other forms of consciousness are derived or extrapolated from "him." All other forms of consciousness, in particular the "souls" of higher forms of life, can thus be said to have been "made in his image." But these embodied and discrete conscious entities (such as ourselves), while derived from a more basic and structural form of consciousness, are yet of a different type; having been constructed from more elemental forms of consciousness, we become a more *defined* type of structure distinct from those elemental compositional forms.

Just as a house is made of wood and bricks, a house is not simply wood, or bricks. We would not point to a house and say, "Look at that wood." Instead, we say, "Look at that house." The house has become a new and unique structure of a specific type, and the wood and bricks are now *part* of the house. The same wood and bricks could just as easily have been used to make another house, and very similar wood and bricks do indeed make other similar houses.

In this manner, we are *internally* derived from a fundamental form of consciousness, yet we bear several distinctions—and our individual distinctness is one of those distinctions. That is, we exhibit a distinguishing aspect of *being*, or a strong degree of individuation—commonly referred to as "the self." We are *not* an undifferentiated form of consciousness, but rather we exist as *very* differentiated and distinct implementations of consciousness.

Perhaps that is unclear. The type of intelligence that we possess is individualized and focused. Embodied, we form a unique manifestation of consciousness that is immersed uniquely within the physical world. We are subject to the maladies and issues that may arise in the body or the world around us, but more importantly, we are capable of direct action *upon* the physical world, and likewise we are capable of actions that may act against maladies of the body.

So, we are a very specialized breed in the realm of consciousness, uniquely immersed within the physical world and uniquely positioned to act upon it—for better or for worse.

The Permeable Membrane

So, are we distant and removed from that more subtle pool of consciousness from which we are derived? Are we distant, cut off, and removed from The-All?

Partly so, it would seem—but perhaps not wholly so. At times it seems as if there is a membrane (to borrow a term from biology) that separates our personal consciousness from the greater and more fundamental form of consciousness. No one denies that there is a subconscious aspect to the mind, a layer beneath which we are unaware, or are, at best, semi-aware. And the subconscious mind represents but one layer. It is one layer which we know exists but that we do not fully perceive or understand. It is a known part of our consciousness that is not fully within our awareness.

Might there be *additional* layers beneath and beyond the mysterious underlying subconscious?

Perhaps the subconscious mind *does* act as a membrane (for lack of a better term) between us and the more fundamental (or perhaps "higher") realms of awareness. At the most fundamental layer, perhaps, resides what we might call "God." If this is so, in a sense we may be semi-connected with our conscious *source* and thereby, in another respect, connected with all other similarly connected beings.

To those who pray, this 'sensation' of connectivity is no mystery. But perhaps we typically perceive this sensation differently regarding prayer. Perhaps when praying, we perceive our prayers as if they are being "listened to" at that time. It is as if our minds, for the duration of the prayers, are being "eavesdropped" upon by a source from above and outside of ourselves.

But when we pray, must we pray out loud, so that "God," from somewhere afar, can literally 'hear' our voices with his physical "ears?" For most of us, no. If and when we pray, we most often pray internally, and we assume that God somehow "hears" those words. If that part of our consciousness that "prays" is not connected somehow *within* to a greater consciousness which "hears" those prayers, by what mechanism do we suppose this interaction occurs?

Reflecting further upon this notion, is it perhaps not the words literally, but the related underlying meanings held within our consciousness that are *directed* toward the subconscious. Is it thus the underlying *meaning* of our words, directed toward the fundamental consciousness via the membrane of subconscious mind, which speaks in its own language to the "Greater Consciousness?" And, as we pray in words, that part of us which 'interfaces' with the deeper consciousness is thereby activated or engaged—uttering in an unknown and more fundamental "tongue" the *deeper meanings* underlying those same words. Perhaps this subconscious part at the "membrane layer" speaks the same "words" that we are speaking in our minds. Via this membrane (perhaps our only form of connection between us and Greater Consciousness), the messages are "translated" into that more fundamental form of communication that exists between us, as an individual conscious being, and God, the most fundamental form of consciousness.

Who can deny that even when we are not "praying," that some interchange is occurring within us, between the highest, most conscious part of ourselves and that part deeper within which is at or beneath the level of our subconscious? Often our thoughts seemingly arise from outside of our awareness, therein to be considered in the full illumination of the conscious mind.

Whether in prayer or not, many times, especially if we "ask," we find that an answer, solution, or inspiration subsequently "occurs" to us. Oddly, the answer is often in the form of a construct or idea that could be said to be "new," in that it is not something we have directly experienced or thought about before. We seemingly 'conjure up' images and dreams that do not represent anything from our own specific personal history.

It is as if one part of the mind "asks" and another part "retrieves"—or perhaps "receives." It is as if a given solution 'bubbles up', as it were, into our higher consciousness; there to be formalized and verbalized as if it were our own. Is this merely the operation of differing parts of the physical brain, or does it perhaps indicate a more subtle interaction between ourselves and something much larger and more fundamental?

Either way, the individual "thinker" has no personal or direct awareness of exactly *how* this interaction occurs across the layers of consciousness within our own minds. Subjectively, we do not really know *how* we think, or the exact mechanics of the process, but we know instinctively 'how to do it', and it just 'happens'.

But most assuredly, within these dialogues— whether they are verbal or nonverbal, whether they occur strictly internally or consist of bouncing ideas across "membranes" and "conscious realms"—therein resides our greatest power and potential. We *are* the thinking form of being. Our inner dialogue provides not only much of our own coloration and rigor of life's journey, but also the greater part of our more advanced accomplishments is derived from the ever-pondering nature of this innermost 'conversation'.

While these interactions and "dialogues" between ourselves and the greater or deeper consciousness occur quite naturally and continuously, it seems this power can be magnified in prayer. In a deliberate act of prayer we normally focus our attention directly on that which matters. In so doing, we often release overly complex problems into the cosmos (or at least release them to a more fundamental part of our own consciousness). We await greater clarity from a source that is subtler and perhaps wiser than that distinct, "higher," and more differentiated portion of ourselves (the individuated self).

While we may share a more basic source-layer of consciousness, we in this world still exist to a strong degree as individuals. Our individuality and capacity as discrete physical beings must be, and is, preserved to a considerable extent. This is important so that the capabilities which enable the types of achievement available to our unique *type* of consciousness (physically embodied), are not rendered incapacitated. So, we necessarily (or with purposeful design) exist somewhat independently, and yet we *do* have some degree of connectivity and continuity with a more elemental type of consciousness; thereby a coalition of interconnectedness is formed among all Life.

How nice and simple it would be, if we could say it is all one way, or all the other, as our logical minds would like to do. But the reality is neither, rather it is some of both, whether we find that conclusion distasteful or not.

Perceive it as a wonderful blending. A permeable "membrane" keeps us individually intact yet receptive to the influx of influences from a more elemental conscious type. We can assume that this is all for the better and that it is a natural part of our ordinary, daily operation of thought.

With confidence in the mechanism and manner of operation of our innermost dialogues, we can assume our own unique roles in the grand symphony of all that is. We can assume our proper orientation with everything, both within and without, knowing that this process of inner dialogue is normal and viable.

Then we can proceed more boldly, perhaps even with great gusto and zeal.

To do so, sooner rather than later, would be wise, for our time in *this* world is surely limited.

The Determination of
the Free-Willed

The dilemma of predestination versus free will is inherent within all philosophical and religious systems. In some cases, the subject is approached openly and wholeheartedly, and one side or the other is ardently espoused and supported. In other belief systems, this glaring conceptual dilemma is merely ignored or overlooked.

Some religious philosophies pin the underlayment of all their principles upon a strict acceptance of the idea of predestination. They believe, in essence, that *all* events were initially set in motion by God, controlled in the present in infinite detail by God, and will be guided to a predetermined conclusion of God's choosing in the future. As such we play but a passive role in such schemas. It becomes difficult for these philosophies to assess or assign personal responsibility (but it doesn't stop them from trying), since any failing can be attributed to the notion that it was unavoidable or "predestined."

At the other extreme, some philosophers argue vehemently against the notion of predestination, at times referencing the random and chaotic principles observable within the universe. They may assert that random factors (set in motion initially at some point of origin), rather than any ordered path govern the net effects of all things. To all actions or activities they observe no rules, and to all outcomes they attribute no intention. They contend in this chaotic worldview, that the net effects of all things are incalculable, and therefore random and without direction.

Additionally, some within the various schools of thought who argue against predeterminism—often those who argue most strongly—insist that, rather than being random or preordained, the thoughts and actions of individual people especially are self-determined. This capacity for self-determination, even if it exists only partially, is often called "free will."

While some philosophies and worldviews may lean toward one extreme or the other regarding predeterminism, many others attempt to dodge the issue entirely. Certainly, some churches, having felt compelled to address the topic in some manner, may have issued a formal doctrine that espouses one point of view or another on the topic. Yet many formal canons scarcely mention it, nor is it ever proudly uttered aloud, and accordingly neither free-will nor predeterminism form any significant part of many denominations' day-to-day teachings.

No one will hear a word of these concepts in a typical Sunday morning sermon. The disposition of a given church on this matter is often strictly symbolic. The topic may have been included in their guiding principles, almost as an afterthought. It is as if they felt including a statement on this topic was obligatory, although distasteful. Or perhaps they needed to establish some point of reference on the topic to settle arguments among their more quizzical adherents.

Regardless of how various churches might weigh in on the subject, in the context of this book, and this world view, one might fairly ask,

"What is the position of Zenithity concerning predestination versus free will?"

To this I might initially answer, "I don't really speak for Zenithity; no one does. It is a theoretical process—although I believe it is, or will be, very real."

The querier might then send a sharp glare and ask again, to which I might answer;

"Probably a combination of free-will and predestination? ...Kinda."

This may come as a bit of a surprise. With discussions of an "inevitable" pathway to an ultimate future (which essentially constitutes Zenithity), one might conclude that everything is considered to be preordained within this philosophy. But that is a little askew from how it was presented, and a bit off from what might be most logical or likely. Zenithity represents the (seemingly contradictory) theoretical possibility that an inevitable pathway to an ultimate future state might certainly develop. In light of the existence of consciousness and the likely morphing and increase of its potential influence over time, it seems *probable* (from some perspectives inevitable) that this pathway to the ultimate will ensue.

However, this is not an absolute certainty. Sitting right here, we cannot say with certitude that this is absolutely so.

Beyond that, a primary tenet of this philosophy is that the living process of Zenithity will reside in the action of Consciousness in its own sense of reasoning and value assessment. There it affects or alters the course of events into the future—and it is expected to do so consistently, successively, and eventually predictably. Over and over again, actions both large and small, committed unintentionally or intentionally by living, breathing conscious entities, will bring Life and the sum of all Consciousness into a state or process of Zenithity (which leads *almost* invariably to a Paradisical future state).

This certainly implies a considerable amount of "free will" that can and will be exerted at every juncture along the way, and in many ways it seems the opposite of *predestination.* In fact one might as easily conclude, that free-will is the very vehicle by which Zenithity arrives.

While the previous statements may contain confusing elements of opposing logic, I believe we will eventually see above and beyond these apparent contradictions, and there will be great union of many of life's seemingly contrasting threads.

So, for Zenithity and the theories surrounding it, the dilemma of free will versus predestination is resolved by abstaining from seeing this as a dilemma at all. They are both true. The process of Zenithity (and The Mechanysis of Perfunction) makes use of our inherent capacity for self-determination as evidenced by that which is achieved via the action of free will. They also make use of the notion that, from another perspective, the net effects of our actions *will lead* to a set of conditions that 'could have been', or might in hindsight appear to be, predetermined.

Zenithity entertains and embraces both free will and predeterminism as differing interpretations of the same sets of data. From an esoteric point of view this difference is perhaps another moot point. For if we arrive at a certain set of conditions upon a timeline, propelled *to* that destination partly by our free will, can we not then say that it was perhaps inevitable that we would have arrived there?

These notions, or the false predicament created by their juxtaposition, may be largely arguments in semantics.

There is indeed much ado over the topic of predestination and much of that topic is simply a literal mess. The ideas of rigid predestination result in yet another form of circular logic. In the larger discussion of life's important issues, this creates a bit of unintentional obfuscation instigated by an elevation of semantics and hyperbole which has been exaggerated to the point of hypocrisy.

So, let us jump off the fence and look at the nature of time and at our own conditions a little closer to home. Looking at our individual timelines, in the immediate present and the near future surrounding our individual state of consciousness, of that state let us say unequivocally:

"Yes, yes. Free will *certainly* exists. We know it to be true from the nature of our own personal experiences. I may choose to take one action or another, and thereby I exert the force of my own conscious self-determination upon my experience, and thereby upon the reality which surrounds me."

Yes, of course, free will exists, and in it resides an explosively vital part of the concept of Zenithity and the surrounding theories.

If a person evaluates a set of choices, and then determines that one of those choices is best for themselves, their family, and those around them, they can then choose to execute or act upon that choice. And, with a little luck, and if that person is adept at overcoming the challenges and meeting the demands required to implement the desired course of action, then presumably, the desired outcome occurs. If it turns out to be a dead end, we can back out, re-evaluate, and try a different approach. But the results are determined *at least partly* by the actions which were at least partly determined by the free-willed process of choice under the guidance of reason. This demonstrates the embodiment of free will, and by example serves as a form of crude definition.

Not only do we *have* free will, but we have some *responsibility* to act. We also have an innate mechanism and motivation to choose and act rightly. Thus, free will is our greatest right, but in so being it becomes our greatest responsibility. For we, and those around us, and those beings in our future that are far greater than us, individually and collectively, will embark upon actions directed by freely chosen, conscious decisions. These actions and decisions will determine our fate and, collectively, the fate of the universe.

It seems that when guided by a consciousness that is motivated toward that which is better (whatever better may be), the inalienable ultimate result would be that which is defined heretofore as Zenithity.

However, let us make it clear, that there are many, many pathways to that conclusion, and perhaps many versions or variations of the process (or state) of Zenithity.

Now, we could go on arguing that the future state did in fact draw us in via the inherent gravity of its value, and in some respects this is true. Equally true, perhaps.

But let us not get mired in the semantics of saying that if a person makes one choice from among many, that even *this* choice was predestined by the sum of all prior events. We could say that even the act of choosing from among varied options is itself an illusion, and that when we make our selection, that selection was itself predetermined by the chain of events of all eternity leading up to the moment of that decision. The birth of that person and all the events within that person's life could be seen as predetermined, and the net effects of all the influences upon that person's life, both internal and external, could be said to result in that single *predetermined* decision.

Now that person may laugh and say, "I changed my mind. I am choosing another option." But then the rigid mindset of predeterminism might say, that this change too, mocking as it were the very nature of "free will," *was likewise predetermined.*

So we begin to see the circular logic of rigid predeterminism. Supporting it becomes the ultimate 'self-fulfilling prophecy' in which there is an 'I told you so' always occurring after the fact.

Thinking in this manner becomes rather pointless. It is barely thinking at all, and it is just rubber stamping, that everything at every step of the way was 'meant to be'.

So, don't get too hung up on predeterminism,
it can always be made to 'seem' right.
The reality is that **consciousness** *is in the driver's seat.*
In the cosmic game of chance, consciousness is the wild card.

So, let's get real; If it smells and tastes of free will, it *is* free will. Where there is smoke, there is fire. We can't be absolved into believing that our actions are moot, rather it is the gainsaying of all choice that is moot. Believing that no matter what is chosen was predetermined is an unrealistic and moot way of thinking and a childish word game in semantics.

Rigid predeterminism is, again, much like a self-fulfilling prophecy, forever locked into a circular form of logic. It consists of an irrational yet irrefutable logic in which, no matter the outcome, one always insists it was meant to be. Thus, proponents of predeterminism will always claim to be right, even though they are really just choosing to believe in this convenient illusion regarding their own infallibility.

Rigid predeterminism is *not* the nature of Zenithity. The process and state of Zenithity, though theoretically inevitable, arrive entirely and precisely because of zillions of free-willed decisions across time and space. And, sadly, not all theoretical roads lead inevitably to Zenithity, even though we believe that the pathway(s) to Zenithity, as navigated by an ever-growing Consciousness, is paradoxically inevitable.

Ah, yes, we should relax, I suppose, and not fume. For paradoxes and apparent contradictions of this nature will become much better understood along the way, as the nature of our consciousness progresses and evolves. What seemed to be contradictory at one juncture of our enlightenment will appear as unity in the next.

Rest assured for now, in this glimpse of what is to come, that predeterminism and free will (as we currently define them) are inextricably intertwined. This intertwined condition, pulsating with a unifying blend of these two polar opposites, best describes *this* place in time, space, and Consciousness in which we now reside.

Why Everything Matters

From our perspective in the here and now, the future seems to be a dilemma wrapped in a paradox. Free will is intertwined somehow with a potentially overshadowing, predetermined fate.

But from that statement, extract if you will, the most relevant portion. The portion having greatest relevance to the individual is *free will*.

From the outside looking in, a casual observer peering down from above might see countless beings scurrying about, performing various actions, and engaging in sometimes repetitive behaviors. If the onlooker somehow possessed knowledge of the Absolute Truth, it might *appear* that each person's behaviors, at every instance, were in fact predetermined.

But, to us, the individuals who are on the inside looking out, it is just the opposite. We *know* that we have free will and are choosing freely from among what seems to be an array of valid conclusions and directions at each and every juncture. This is the perspective with which *you* were endowed. The other perspective is, for practical purposes, a fantasy.

> *From our personal perspectives,*
> *we do indeed possess free will,*
> *and thus we exert considerable influence.*
> *We must remember to act accordingly.*

From this perspective, we even have some *responsibility* to freely choose that which is best, or at least the better from among the available options, for as conscious beings we learn quickly that our choices have consequences.

"Consequences" is not a word to fear, although we sometimes do. Consequences are not always bad, nor are they always good, but clearly our choices almost always have *consequences*, which are typically of a magnitude proportionate to the relevance of the choice being made.

As conscious beings inhabiting the physical world, we learn quickly of cause and effect, and of our own roles in this all-important process.

Let us take a different route, in short fashion, through the topic of the previous chapter.

Every philosophical framework, and every religion, must struggle with notions regarding predetermination. The question is, "Is the course of everything set, or not?"

In the philosophical framework loosely presented within this book, the course *is* expected to be set or fixed (comparatively) during Zenithity, but there is still randomness, free will, and choice of action; these are in accordance with how these things *should* be in an ultimate state. But leading up to Zenithity, there is a *greater degree* of randomness and uncertainty—hence the role of free will is heightened. This inherent uncertainty will be navigated artfully by Consciousness, and via the action of free will. The circumstances will be navigated and mitigated by the act of consciousness, after careful evaluation, then applying conscious action (cause), yielding the appropriate result (effect)—over and over again.

Then I imagine, some people, listening but never quite hearing, will still be heard saying, "If *everything* is set concerning the course or pathway to Zenithity, then nothing really matters, since all is set and there is nothing we can do about it."

Perhaps I have been very unclear, and for that I apologize.

All things matter, and the course leading up to the end is _not set_.

Let's take a different and more positive tack.

Let us start with this assumption:

It was always true from the beginning of time that everything would arrive, at the end of time, at a perfect and most highly evolved state. Since time has no beginning nor ending, the concept of the "end of time" is used figuratively. The point is that Consciousness, embedded within space and time where change is possible, will inevitably arrive at an "utmost state" (or a state which is nearly equivalent); this is due to Consciousness's own influence and self-determination over time.

What varies considerably is the potential course of events taken, the details of the journey itself, how long it will take, and perhaps even the consistency of the "final" state; these are *not set*. It is the sheer act of reckoning—by the combined consciousness of all beings—that steers the course and duration of this journey. As people today are fond of stating, "It is more about the journey than the destination." At our current position on the timeline, this is perhaps the most accurate summary.

Also, nowhere has it been concluded that every society, every planet, every people, will *arrive* at the final destination. Certainly, some will falter and fall by the wayside. And some civilizations will languish for millennia in darkness, consumed with wars, pestilence, and all manner of consequences derived from the ill-fated lack of inspiration and improper reasoning by the populace and the powers that be.

While there are many times in history when our own planet (Earth) has essentially gone "retrograde," in general it can be seen that progress has been made, albeit gradually—despite all the distractions. It is as if we are now at a stage wherein we take one step back for every two steps forward. Progress seems slow. We often miscalculate and suffer from the consequences of our poor choices, and we are frequently burned by our own mishandling of the cause-and-effect process. The human species and its society are in need of countless upgrades or enhancements, but these seem to be slow in coming or are not apparent on the horizon.

Yet, hopefully, over time, we learn. And in due time, the better of our instincts and our reasoning will prevail. Can we not see, despite our current set of problems, the overall rapidly ascending arc of human development?

Our development is not all physical nor does it all occur within our societies. There has been a learning and growing process within the very awareness of man. It can be said that this internal state of awareness too has morphed, evolved, or progressed—even more rapidly than the physical form that it inhabits.

That is not to say that we could not, at some juncture, devolve or digress. Progress could surely evaporate at any significant juncture, due to an unforeseen impetus. This is clearly within the realm of possibility.

For that matter, we could all eliminate one another—and all Life on this planet—at some horribly inconceivable juncture in the future. This too is possible, no doubt.

But even if so, the greater consciousness that is certainly pervading the universe will prevail, and hopefully there will not be so much stupidity across the *entire* realm of the conscious universe.

One would like to think that we would *not* self-destruct, and moreover, that we would survive and thrive. It would be amazing to know of the incredible state of awareness we as humans will eventually attain.

All of this is within the realm of Zenithity. All of this is possible during, or even before, the period anticipated as the Mechanysis of Perfunction has distinctly begun.

This is all to say, by the long way around, that our decisions and our actions *do matter*. On an individual scale our decisions matter within our personal spheres of influence. These also contribute in some small measure to an increase (or decrement) in our net progress toward a state of Zenithity.

And in collective assemblies—like families, groups, organizations, societies, and nations—the net effects of our decisions and actions are correspondingly magnified for ourselves, one another, and other societies or nations. This trend is expected to persist and amplify throughout the course of The Mechanysis of Perfunction.

While there is real risk to this approach, there is a corresponding need for a certain type of faith. This is not a blind faith that despite whatever acts of ineptitude or callousness we may perform we will magically "land on our feet." Nor is it a blind faith which asserts that we may languish eternally in any degree of imperfection, wallowing in pain and suffering, only then to somehow arise without effort, unscathed, from the great hells that we have endured.

Faith resides in the notion that the whole of Life *will* eventually or gradually "get it" and what is not good, progressively gives way to what is *better*. As we endure all manner of ups and downs, progress and enlightenment will occur. And surely, God, to the extent that he has a face, surely smiles upon our progress.

This is inevitable, but before the inevitable is a "pre-inevitable" state in which we become more gradually "locked into" a more calculated and deliberate process. That process as it tapers and leads directly into Zenithity embodies a nearly inescapable act of progressing toward "perfection" - whatever it is that perfection may be.

But we must get there first.

And we must have faith—in our reasoning, in the Consciousness that pervades all things, and in the God who awaits us in paradise at the end of time—that we will navigate our course incrementally to the best of destinations and destinies. The process will be wrought with failures and setbacks initially, but for these, all is forgiven—especially if we have *intended* to follow the best path.

Some will say that it is just as likely that, if guided by consciousness, we will all go spiraling off into fear and darkness. A huge calamity will occur - a hell of sorts. It's surely possible, I must concede. And people are free to believe in that dystopian vision if they want to. And in a worse case scenario, I presume everything could and would reset or rebound eventually.

Others may say that we will just as likely remain forever locked into a state of stasis, caught somewhere between positive and negative and forever stuck in a balance where nothing ever really progresses significantly. It's certainly possible, for sure. At least for a time being. And anyone may choose to believe this, especially if it somehow serves them to do so.

Some people simply *hate this chapter*, which implies that "everything matters." Some would prefer to believe instead in the mantra that "nothing matters." It seems that there are many who are so weary and would like to believe that *noth-*

ing they think, or say, or do really matters. Because, if things really *do matter,* everyone would then have to exert a degree of mental (and physical) effort and take some responsibility.

Subconsciously, those who choose to believe that "nothing matters," allow themselves to *feel* as if they don't have to worry about anything, and they assume no responsibility toward anything whatsoever. It is a form of mental laziness, which can form in response to our minds being overloaded and thus made weary. Under these conditions, many tired minds will choose nihilism (an attitude that "nothing matters") because it is "easier" and requires little or no mental effort.

In an oddly related way, the eagerness with which some people embrace the idea of absolute predestination is based upon that same underlying desire to comfortably assume that "nothing matters." The attraction, for some people regarding predeterminism is the same as the attraction that some have to nihilism: they both allow us to *assume* that nothing we do matters and therefore we need not have a worry or a care. It just feels "easier" that way.

But *I* contend that we will forever be destined for an ultimate positive state. Above and beyond that, I further contend that over time, and regardless of any beliefs or efforts to the contrary, *this* belief will overrun *their* beliefs—or the lack of any beliefs whatsoever.

Eventually the ignorance and negativity will die out. Why?

Because Consciousness makes a difference and consciousness can choose.

At times, the positive influence of consciousness may seem to make only a minor difference, and it may take a while for the mass rot of cynical gloom to fully slough off. But the philosophies of helplessness, of doom and gloom, will be forgotten in due time, simply eclipsed and quietly archived into some very old and dusty books of amusingly arcane history.

Resolution, Born of Consequence Chain

Whether you believe that there is Consciousness outside of the physical or that consciousness exists only within our physical bodies, *either way,* I contend that the process of Zenithity will occur.

Either way.

Whether conceived by a primordial God, or merely the result of latter-day lifeforms that have spontaneously arisen and evolved from the mire:

Zenithity will occur.

Either way.

And on that note, why can't we recognize that Consciousness *could* or does exist outside what we call the physical world? It is in fact our physical world that is the impossible, the more improbable, the outlier.

Who says that consciousness as we know it can't exist in any form but within the physical world? Even if consciousness of the type we know were limited to the physical world, might consciousness of a form entirely unknown to us exist in another realm beyond our physical reality?

It is the physical world that is more improbable than the more ethereal conscious world. If one might exist without the other, the conscious realm (in being more subtle than hard matter) might appear the more independent of the two. The conscious element, in its transcendent independence, possibly subordinates and dominates the physical. Perhaps the physical is a creation or emanation of a greater form of consciousness. Thus the physical state, although very real, may be secondary to (as descending from) a greater form of Consciousness.

But I will assume, that for *most* of us (even those not quite as skeptical as myself), that seeing is believing. So until we see or otherwise experience an incorporeal form of consciousness, we have a justifiable right to conclude that such things may not exist. Fair enough.

Finally, in the end, this too is neither here nor there—it is what it is.

Why?

Because Zenithity *will* occur.

Either way.

But the consequences of our choices, along the way, could be staggeringly dramatic.

For better or worse, the consequences, along the way, *will be* decidedly significant.

Hopefully, the consideration and growing awareness of these subjects will lead us individually into more deliberate and increasingly better states within our own personal spheres of existence—today and always.

Consequence, Responsibility, and Purpose

So, if it is not yet clear, that which we think, say, and do *actually matter* because there are *always* consequences. Every action we take propels into motion a set of results for which we are responsible (knowingly or not).

In this way, if we remain pleasantly focused upon the matters before us, Life becomes a purposeful process that seems relevant in this moment and into the next, continuing from one day to the next. The notions of meaning or purpose (or the potential for lack thereof) do not arise in this state, as we are utterly immersed in purpose and its presence is self-evident.

This sense of purpose is not meant to be false, derived, or artificial. It is not meant to be a relentlessly driven pursuit of an inflexible set of ideals. Instead, we thrive best within a sense of calm and natural purposefulness, grounded in our own day-to-day existence, our personal growth, our relationships, and our accomplishments.

We feel best when our thoughts and actions feel effortless and successful—like they were meant to be. Feeling that this moment is truly "meant to be" contains a certain magic that allows us to best enjoy and fulfill it. In adapting to the ever-changing moment and exerting our best state of mind upon it we become "one with the moment" and perhaps even "one with the universe."

In this calm and purposeful way, we exist without undue pressure or concern. We become our best selves, always and forever reinvented in the moment. In this way, we are always reinventing it too. Reinventing the moment that is, our circumstances, and the present state of affairs. Our core consciousness is best expressed in the fluidity of this approach.

While many conclusions regarding Zenithity and related philosophies may seem esoteric or abstract, they illustrate or illuminate a set of facts that represent a practical and positive set of truths. These conceptual ideas can spill over into countless pragmatic ancillary ideas. Ideas of this sort can be further translated into action and practice and thereby into the world of results and benefits.

From the framework that has been summarized herein, one can easily derive additional sets of more pragmatic philosophies that can be used day by day. The theories regarding Zenithity do not constitute a philosophical "bubble" within which all things reside only in a world of thoughts, beliefs, and theories. Instead, they constitute a platform or launching pad from which corollary ideas and practices can arise. New fields of thought thus spawned may hopefully be more pragmatic, while also residing in closer concordance with a greater Truth.

In this way, may our ideas moving forward more clearly resonate with the Greater Consciousness.

A Springboard for
Practical Belief Systems

The theories behind and surrounding Zenithity represent a viable and likely valid set of ideas which, if ex-
plored, could yield an array of practical positive pathways to
enhance the success of individuals and societies. This becomes especially clear when comparing Zenithity to many
other prevalent philosophies and belief systems.

For example, the bulk of extant belief systems (especially
religious ones) are fraught with illogical inconsistency, fan-
tastically unbelievable fables, and, in many respects, are 'out
of touch' with any but the most ancient of peoples.

And, outside of religion, what do we have that is cohe-
sive? What do we have that may guide and unify our various
highly specialized pursuits, and disciplines? What will nurture, encourage, and support us without leaving us puzzled
concerning fables which are presented that seem rather out-

landish and are most likely spurious? Huge swaths of people feel a growing aversion to the outright 'kookiness' of many aspects of the existing religions, yet in rejecting these ancient ramblings, they find that there is nothing of meaningful substance to fill the void.

Worse still, many of the existing non-religious philosophies and belief systems are seething with all flavors of self-destructive negativity. Others are packed with paralyzing nonsense and irrational fantasy, while failing to provide any positive or practical contribution to our experience of reality. Often the secular philosophies are lacking in any encouraging, uplifting, or beneficial teachings.

A philosophy is bane if it leads us nowhere, and inspires us to nothing.

Where stifling negativity is lacking, and absurd fantasy is amiss, we find that only a few semi-viable, overarching belief systems remain. Those remaining few often have little or nothing to offer of any practical or inspirational value.

In our search for belief systems and worldviews which can serve humanity in a logical and helpful manner, it is fully acceptable and perhaps wise that we might sample and review many of the existing philosophical schools of thought. However, we might wish to do so in a careful manner – like sticking a toe into the muddy waters before plunging in headfirst. For many belief systems are little more than entangling distractions – seemingly paralyzing or poisoning us. Thus they can rob us of our valuable time and can cloud the clarity of our vision. By harboring defeatist or illogical beliefs, we sully or weaken the potential viability of our actions. Even if but for a while, unnecessary distractions are best minimized. So we may need to more quickly plow through certain unyielding and known impediments, thus avoiding some obvious dead-ends along the way.

In order to travel nimbly and lightly, we will need to divest ourselves of a large parcel of the most negative baggage we have accumulated collectively and individually. We may need to confront and dispense with the most irrational and destructive ideas more directly, and the sooner the better. Ideas which are both false and also malicious must be not only resisted, but openly challenged, defeated, and ultimately discarded (except perhaps for a fading reference in the historical record).

One might say we must debunk a bunch of negative junk.

We may need to do a lot of unloading and dumping.

Let's start with these . . .

Saying Goodbye to Doomsday Death Cults

Sadly, a large number of adherents of several of the world's religions (past and present) seem to have 'latched on' to negative "prophecies" or teachings that glorify the destruction of this world and the damnation of humanity. From these viewpoints a dark worldview arises in which nothing good is ever worth doing. In these dour and harshly judgmental circles, nothing matters except waiting for the grand obliteration of Earth with all its 'sin and woe.'

Thankfully, there is one tiny consolation if the doomsday cults are one day proven right; the long-awaited cataclysm will also silence, once and for all, the pitiful aches and moans of all the lovers of damnation and doom.

Astonishingly, in modern times, significant segments within a few of the world's leading religions have lost sight of "the big picture." They have thrown brotherly love out the window. They have only hatred for all of God's creation, and they may cite some ancient damning cryptic text as justification for their illogical conclusions. In so doing, they have become little more than sad twisted death cults. Regardless of their religion of origin, their focus is always similar and seems to arise from a miserable disenchantment with life.

It's always the same story – or a similar variation:

A vengeful "god" will finally say (and very soon of course), "I've had it with these sapiens!" And then this childishly angry "god" will violently destroy his own "broken" creation. Then with his broken creatures burning in eternal damnation, he can spin up a *new* creation that will "somehow" be more appealing to the perpetually sad denizens of the doom-and-gloom breakfast club.

Never do the doomsday believers conclude, nor even pause to consider, that it is perhaps *this* reality that moves forward into the future to ultimately *become* that long-awaited paradise spoken of in tales of old. They can't seem to imagine a paradise arriving in due time via gradual progress in *this* world. They can't imagine God working *through* the human species and *through* his own creation to achieve his ultimate goals.

Never do they conclude that God's creation, regardless of how 'broken' *they* perceive it to be, is not theirs to damn or judge as "unworthy." *This* reality is God's creation; through *this* reality will arise the ultimate reality (Heaven).

Before we get there, these childish, angry, unforgiving depictions of "god" will begin to fade long before we rise to a spiritually higher state.

Goodbye to Doomsday Science Mongers Too!

Aside from these "doomsday religious cults" (which are thankfully waning in numbers and influence within the more educated societies), there are many other people who are still very entrenched in an overtly negative worldview concerning the future. For instance, a large swath of frightened and timid persons might categorize our future as being fraught primarily with menacing challenges. Those engaged heavily in such thinking perceive the future in terms of ever more frightening and insurmountable problems whose complexity (and potential for disaster) only increases as time and civilization advance.

As was stated earlier, a healthy dose skepticism is good to have.

...I said a "*healthy*" dose.

Not an overdose.

Even outside of religious "prophecy," there are those who might "scientifically" espouse the belief that mankind is "doomed" or that somehow humanity—or all of life, or even all of reality—is somehow fatally flawed. Sadly, while often well intentioned, they often allow these doom-and-gloom philosophies to influence their demeanor and their own outlook on life. Our thought processes have become chock-full of negative projections that we cast not only upon the future, but also upon the present, and on the human race in general. In so doing we (or they) are basically encasing *everything* in the sickly *goo* of negative expectations, perceptions, and projections.

Even if we refuse to echo or spew the narrative of downerism, there is a dark undertow to this form of "philosophical gossip" whose negativity is difficult to avoid. Sometimes we are forced to swim in these stagnant pools of negativity, even though we know it is wrong (or unhealthy) to do so – even though we are attempting to rise above. The downward pull of this philosophical gossip makes it difficult for those of us who would choose to swim rather than sink.

We consume this garbage from birth, and of course it takes its toll.

So, just saying (again), a little unloading and dumping couldn't hurt.

Perhaps one day, the doomsday worshipers and cheerleaders (whether religious or secular in origin) will fade into obscurity. Until then, perhaps they too serve a purpose; inspiring us to be keenly vigilant regarding the correctness of our actions as we navigate the future.

In fairness, we should not make too much light of the deep and often foreboding problems that man has already faced and overcome. Nor should we attempt to oversimplify or gloss over the challenges and setbacks we might face going forward.

However, it is a primary conclusion of the well-reasoned theories proposed in this book, that for mankind— moreover for life, intelligent life—and for reality as a whole (The-All):

There is no predetermined or inescapable "doomsday"

And while it may be somewhat flawed,

reality contains no inherently damnable "fatal flaw."

If somehow, these presumptions turn out to be false,

(and I must certainly leave that determination to God and fate)

I will never rejoice in the destruction of God's good creation.

And never, will I ever harm one hair on the head of any of God's children.

Especially not in the name of God.

And by the way, we are all God's children.

And no caring child of God would ever idly watch another's soul burn in eternity.

Thus, I will never smile contentedly over the damnation of a single soul.

Nor will I embrace a belief that promotes such a damning view of God.

There is a positive and future-forward mindset, which we must begin to cultivate. It encourages the anticipation or expectation of expansiveness, solutions, enhancements, and advancement. A positive worldview of this type espouses that Life has within itself the seeds of a greater reality: the capability of progressively envisioning and achieving an ever-greater state. In another relevant context, via the flexible nature of consciousness, we are embedded with the pattern and instructions for approximating an ultimate state.

It can be easily seen that mankind always has (and always will) overcome important challenges and, in so doing, he typically arrives at a higher, more advanced, or advantageous state. In essence, in the process of overcoming our most significant problems, a welcome resultant that often occurs is a net enhanced state of existence. The enhancement appears to be generated whenever we fully exercise our immense problem-solving capabilities. In some scenarios our efforts and capacities extend over, above, and beyond the mere elimination or correction of the original offending issue. Coinciding with the embetterment of our conditions is an embetterment or enhancement of our state of awareness;

In overcoming challenges, our state of mind thus evolves in a positive manner.

Practical Belief Systems and Healthy Principles

It is beyond the scope and intention of this work to enumerate every possible belief system or principle that is in accord with (or in opposition to) the ideas and ideals summarized or introduced in this brief book.

But there is a sense of hopefulness inherent within the ideas and philosophies surrounding the theory of Zenithity and the related concepts. From the conceptual ideas depicted herein, a loose framework is established. From this framework, which I hope might be inspiring to a humble but cherished few, any number of practical or advantageous belief systems and related endeavors might be launched.

At a minimum, I would like to believe that we will be more proactive and selective in our beliefs and ideals moving forward. Hopefully, moving forward, the belief systems we *choose* will be increasingly more accurate and in line with the best of our inclinations.

May the best of our innermost potential be forever unleashed.

The Summation of Expectation

The ideas, beliefs, and theories presented in this book might be seen as loosely forming the framework of a philosophy. For lack of a better term, we can call this new philosophy;

The Theories Surrounding the Principle of Zenithity

Or, for short;

The Theory of Zenithity

Constituting this theoretical framework, the following bulleted statements summarize individual and semi-related conclusions which are not necessarily presented in any specific order.

Also, it is not necessary for *all* of the conditions to be true for any (or some) of them to be considered or rendered true. In other words, many of the expectations expressed are independent conclusions which *generally* support (or might predict) the others.

Since many of these conclusions are expectations regarding the future, they may be difficult or impossible to ascertain or prove until the future has transpired (or at least a portion of it). As such, the conclusions are more philosophically reasoned rather than scientifically observable, and they should therefore be evaluated with reason and logic. For topics where empiricism is necessarily lacking, we must use both heart and mind to evaluate, navigate, or validate any idea for its value, truth, and merit.

Let us not forget, that *reason* is, and has always been, our primary means of assessing newly acquired information.

Here are some of the fundamental conclusions (or expectations) of this framework, presented in bullet form and without any of my typical intervening prose or poetry:

- Consciousness exists more undeniably than any other form of reality.
- A form of Consciousness may have predated all other forms of reality (and the associated phenomenon), such as space (matter), or time (events).
- A form of Consciousness which predated all other forms of reality, might have created or played a role in inducing those forms into existence.
- Regardless of its origin, the *existence* of Consciousness is the most significant and highly advanced aspect of reality.
- Consciousness exerts itself, and thereby affects reality and the course of future events.
- Consciousness can and will adapt and evolve into ever higher *forms* of Consciousness or Conscious Life.
- Consciousness not only learns of details and facts, but also develops new *types or modes* of intelligence and

awareness which may arise seemingly in the form of upgrades or enhancements.

- As it achieves higher and more effective states, Consciousness becomes increasingly dominant over space (matter) and time (events).

- From the perspective of Consciousness, all possibilities form a qualitative hierarchy (or "ladder") of "worse to better" comparative conceptual conditions, This ladder of conceptual conditions is of infinite proportion in either direction.

- Since Consciousness is selective, and has the capacity to learn, it will *generally* (over time) navigate the "ladder" in ascending order. (The Principle of Proportionate Good.)

- As Consciousness amends reality (and itself) in a progressively auspicious manner, an ultimate positive direction or course is established which leads toward an infinitely ascendant good. (The Theorem of Ultimate Good)

- Consciousness, by existing, by exerting bearing, and by having selectivity, will ultimately tend toward an inevitable and absolute state encompassing all positive states. (The Process/State of Zenithity)

Further Supportive or Elaborative Concepts:

- The ultimate state or process of Zenithity might be seen as a form of "paradise", "heaven", or "utopia".
- Prior to the achievement of this ultimate state/process, we will find ourselves (along with other conscious entities that may exist) in a semi-deliberate preparatory state/process. (The Mechanysis of Perfunction)
- Prior to the state/process which leads to Zenithity, we find ourselves in a state of growing awareness and we begin to witness and experience the rudimentary origins of an existence with a positive future forward focus. (The Awakening Dawn)
- In the earlier (and latter) states, our personal experiences reside nonetheless along the "ladder" described by The Principle of Proportionate Good.
- Our beliefs, choices, and actions allow us to navigate reality in the present via a series of cause-and-effect scenarios.
- Our individual and cumulative actions basically constitute a deliberate or unintentional navigation gradually upwards on the Ladder of Proportionate Good.
- We reside consistently within the present, and our perpetual actions within the present affect the consistency of the present state for us locally or individually.
- Our actions within the present may also intentionally or unintentionally affect future states of the present, for better or worse.

- The demonstrable effects of a person's actions upon his/her present state and the ensuing future illustrate the cause-effect relationship of consciousness upon reality (albeit on a smaller scale and in a more limited localized manner).

- It can be seen that consciousness exerts an element of free will, and will likely continue to do so as this would be part of an ultimate or idealized state of conditions.

- The ultimate state, being the result of a series of self-directed actions arising from a body of conscious entities (or from a Greater Consciousness), demonstrates that free will is, in fact, the vehicle of Zenithity.

- Despite exerting free will and self-determination, it can be seen that an ultimate state/process exists, which being inevitable, implies or describes a form of predetermination.

- It is believed that the seeming paradox of free will versus preordination will eventually be resolved as we become more able to comprehend dichotomies or apparent contradictions.

- Consciousness, space (matter), and time (events) can be seen as the Three Pillars of Reality (or three dimensions). Of the 3, consciousness can be seen as having ascendancy or greater relevance.

- Of the 3 Pillars of Reality, it is only via consciousness that we apprehend the other two (space/matter, time/events).

- The expectations described here were not derived from ancient scriptures or prophecies, but rather by applying consciousness and reason toward the analysis or awareness of the future.
- The ideas of absolute damnation, an angry "god", a fatally flawed nature of reality, or an unavoidable "doomsday" (whether of scriptural or scientific origin) are rejected as contrary and counterproductive to the good and wholesome expectations of this philosophy and the beings it serves.
- There is an inherent worth in the self, the soul, and any being representing an element of higher consciousness (including all human beings).
- It is illogical to assume that a benevolent creator levies eternal damnation due to the humble actions of simple beings who were created.
- While beliefs that assign unforgivable guilt are invalid in the extreme, at the other extreme, any belief system which completely eliminates *any* personal responsibility is misguided, lazy, and counterproductive.
- What we think, say, and especially what we *do* as individuals, truly matter, so nihilism and absolute predeterminism are rejected.
- All problems are surmountable and will ultimately be solved, eliminated, or conquered.
- Greater Consciousness (the force having the most important net affect upon the nature of reality over time) can be considered to be the sum of; human consciousness (as an extension of any Godlike conscious-

ness that may exist), along with any Godlike form of consciousness (that may exist), as well as any other higher forms of consciousness (that may exist within the universe, be they physically embodied or incorporeal).

- If a Greater Consciousness (in the form of a primordial God) exists, we are considered to be derived or descended from Him. Thus, we most likely consist of a *similar* elemental form of consciousness, even though we are decidedly more individualized and localized (in such a way that we may act upon the physical).

- If a Greater Consciousness (in the form of a primordial God) exists, we surely share the common bond and destiny with Him. We have shared interests and are decidedly "on the same side".

- If a Greater Consciousness (in the form of a primordial God) does not (or did not) originally exist, the net *sum* of consciousness, especially as we approach Zenithity, may still potentially become a "Godlike" form of Greater Consciousness.

- Our worth as individual beings will be heightened as Life becomes more greatly understood and appreciated in concert with our progress through higher states of awareness.

- Numerous elements of Truth will be more keenly understood moving forward, which will yield an ongoing "leveling up" in the form of enhancements or upgrades to our conscious states (and physical/societal states).

- An acceleration in the understanding of Absolute Truth is likely to occur at some stage in our future. This enhanced awareness of all things will allow us to become more aware of our direction and our impacts upon future events and conditions.
- The deliberate study of Consciousness as it impacts Reality, and the potential future states which could exist, will emerge and further facilitate our benevolent advancement. (Futurology)
- It is hoped that these ideas (in their existing or amended forms), aside from them being found valid or accurate, will be foundationally inspiring or encouraging to many others (ideas), and to many other people.
- (Add your own thoughts, conclusions, reflections, or expectations here.)

Ever Boldly Forward

When we have wiped the sleep from our eyes, it becomes clear that our journey is one of unyielding expansion and development. It is a thrilling journey that leads to destinations having inconceivable yet soaring potential.

Our ancestors once navigated the journey of our people through time, unaided by the layers upon layers of incremental knowledge and skills that we have acquired. Truly, we are standing upon the shoulders of giants.

But in the future, we will exist as an even greater people, perhaps as an even greater *form* of being. We will reside in perpetually advancing types of civilizations, having more highly evolved and progressively enhanced forms of awareness.

As we reach for the stars (literally and figuratively), we may encounter other advanced forms of Life that are likewise involved in this journey of Greater Consciousness.

In hindsight, most of us from today's world would have been ill-equipped to survive and prevail against the rigors faced by our ancient predecessors. Those challenges required a different type of strength and cunning. We will always remain eternally grateful to them, for lucky are we in *this* day, that they so doggedly prepared the way for us though history's more difficult and trying times.

But just as those who came before us, we will rise to the occasion to meet and overcome whatever challenges may arise. The future is *our* domain, and we will adapt to it, and as needed we will forge it into whichever form that is idealized by The-All. Forever evolving and with our circumstances ever progressing, our descendants will become greater beings than we. They will live in worlds far richer in experience than any of which we have ever imagined.

While we cannot be certain of the exacting details of these circumstances, nor of how they will unfold, we can be relatively certain that, in the course of time, these types of occurrences will become increasingly common;

as Consciousness wills it to be so.

The Fundamental
Worthiness of Life

We should each of us be aware that residing within is a fundamentally good and worthwhile being—exactly as he or she was created by The-All.

This applies to each of us individually, to ourselves, and to each person that we encounter.

Stated more personally and directly:

Be aware that *you* are essentially a good person, and that the essence, which is at the core of "yourself," is fundamentally good.

Find and cherish the essence of good within, and nurture it so that it might grow and shine ever more brightly.

Strive to find within others this same core-essence of good, even though it may be more difficult to recognize it within another than within ourselves.

In moments of anger toward any other person, recall that *they* too were once some mother's baby. A child who has grown and matured, yes, but somewhere within still a child.

As we are all raised up from innocence into the world of the broken, can we so easily judge or place blame?

Find Love and acceptance for all persons, if by any means you possibly can.

There is an innate and fundamental goodness and worthiness to Life itself, the Self, and The-All.

While each of these is flawed, they are all drawn to a destination that is elevated and toward an ideal which is unflawed.

Each of us arose from a species that is flawed or imperfect.

That species arose from a set of conditions that were imperfect.

The-All, in primordial infancy, gave rise to a universe that was basically flawed and imperfect.

Yet, there is incredible goodness, greatness, and worthiness permeating all of it.

And no degree of imperfection can ever invalidate the most awesome nature of The-All.

Yet greater still is the ultimate good toward which all things are incessantly drawn.

This is Zenithity.

www.ingramcontent.com/pod-product-compliance
Lightning Source LLC
Chambersburg PA
CBHW070549130626
46556CB00001B/78